Manuscript Sources in the Rosenberg Library

Manuscript Sources

IN THE

Rosenberg Library

A SELECTIVE GUIDE

EDITED BY

JANE A. KENAMORE AND MICHAEL E. WILSON

Published for the
ROSENBERG LIBRARY
by the
TEXAS A&M UNIVERSITY PRESS
COLLEGE STATION

Library of Congress Cataloging in Publication Data

Rosenberg Library.
Manuscript sources in the Rosenberg Library.

Includes index.
1. Texas—History—Manuscripts—Catalogs.
2. Texas—History—Sources—Bibliography—Catalogs.
3. Rosenberg Library—Catalogs. I. Kenamore,
Jane A. (Jane Allen), 1938– . II. Wilson,
Michael E. (Michael Edward), 1949–   . III. Title.
Z1339.R74   1983   [F386]   016.9764   82–45896
ISBN 0–89096–146–8

Manufactured in the United States of America
FIRST EDITION

Contents

Illustrations

Preface

SCHOLARS have long known the Rosenberg Library as custodian of certain key manuscript collections pertaining to early Texas. The papers of Samuel May Williams, secretary to Stephen F. Austin; James Morgan, commandant of Galveston Island in 1836–37; and Gail Borden, early customs officer for the Port of Galveston, have attracted historians of colonial and republican Texas. Civil War scholars have gleaned information from the "J.O.L.O. Log," a record of naval activity off Galveston in 1861; the letters of Jeremiah Y. Dashiell, inspector general of Texas during the Civil War; and miscellaneous correspondence describing life during the bloody conflict.

The need to provide more detailed information regarding manuscripts in the Rosenberg Library became apparent during a recent period of growth in our holdings. Since 1977, new acquisitions and the elimination of a processing backlog have accounted for a sixfold increase in manuscripts accessible for research. As a result of the growth, the old collections so familiar to Texas historians now account for a small percentage of manuscripts in the library; and the focus of our holdings has shifted from antebellum political history to nineteenth- and twentieth-century social and economic history of the Gulf Coast region.

Preserving the past is not a new activity for the Rosenberg Library. The oldest public library in Texas in continuous operation, the Rosenberg is the successor institution to the Galveston Mercantile Library founded in 1871. Through a bequest from Henry Rosenberg—immigrant, banker, and self-proclaimed capitalist—the present library opened its doors in 1904; and from the beginning, the institution was the repository for manuscripts reflecting early Texas history.

The roots of the Rosenberg Library as manuscripts repository lie in the Galveston Historical Society, predecessor to the Galveston Historical Foundation known nationally for its work in architectural preservation. A dozen men founded the society in 1871 to preserve the unique history of Texas, which in the words of the society "was filled with shining examples of human activity and notable records of virtue and of crime." For nearly a decade the organization actively collected manuscripts, maps, books, pamphlets, and newspapers that reflected the history of the state. An indication of the group's success was the publication of a pamphlet for the annual meeting in 1876. Ashbel Smith gave the keynote address, "Reminiscences of the Texas Republic," which the society printed along with a list of its archival holdings. Collections included the papers of James Morgan, early Galveston and Texas newspapers, Freedmen's Bureau circulars, and Joseph McCutchan's diary of the Mier expedition, as well as maps, photographs, and books on Texas.

Although the Galveston Historical Society had an active beginning, interest in the organization waned in the 1880s. In 1894, the group reorganized under a new name, the Texas Historical Society of Galveston. After the society nearly lost its historical collections in the Hurricane of 1900, the group voted to move the papers into the Rosenberg Library; and the board of directors of the library agreed to store the materials. In 1931, after the society had ceased to meet on a regular basis, the organization donated the collections to the library.

Although the Galveston Historical Society preceded the Rosenberg Library as collector of manuscripts, the library has actively sought historical materials since it opened. Under the leadership of the first librarian Frank C. Patten (1904–34), the library solicited historical documents. In 1922, Patten circulated a brochure that noted:

Galveston was the center of things in Texas for many years, and of overshadowing importance to the whole region, and there is a large amount of most interesting and dramatic material that should be collected as a record for the future historian. Those having Galveston or Texas historical matter are invited to consider the desirability of turning it all over to the Rosenberg Library . . . to be added to our local historical collections before [the material] is scattered, lost, or destroyed.

As a result of the publicity, the library acquired several significant collections. Among the most notable were the papers of Samuel May Williams and J. C. League, land speculator.

While the library acquired valuable material, it lacked the staff and space to process manuscript collections and house them in areas of public access. Most of the documents went into storage in the building's multileveled attic. For years, access to the holdings was only through librarians familiar with the papers and the people who created them; and the staff willingly hauled the heavy boxes out of the attic for researchers to use.

The turning point in the history of the Rosenberg Library as manuscripts repository occurred in 1967. Under the leadership of John W. Harris, chairman of the board of directors, the library launched a campaign to build a wing that would more than double the size of the building. Receiving major funding from the Moody Foundation and smaller gifts from citizens in Galveston, the new facilities opened in 1971. The board allocated over five thousand square feet of space in the new building to the Archives Department.

Six years after the Moody wing opened, the National Historical Publications and Records Commission funded a project to process the manuscript collections so long in storage. By July, 1979, the staff had arranged and described over 650 linear shelf feet of material. Collections processed under the grant include the papers of J. C. League (1863–1929), H. M. Trueheart (1859–1909), Texas State Senator A. R. Schwartz (1964–80), Representative Ed J. Harris (1963–76), the Rotary Club of Galveston (1913–76), the Galveston Art League (1914–46), the Galveston Little Theatre (1921–53), the Galveston Equal Suffrage Association (1912–20), and many others.

Just after the library completed the NHPRC project, the Archives Department acquired its largest and probably most significant collection to date—the papers of H. Kempner, unincorporated (1870–1969). The papers of this longtime Galveston firm contain records of cotton, banking, sugar, and insurance interests based in the Texas Gulf Coast region. Under a project funded by H. Kempner, the Archives Department completed processing and indexing the collection in the fall of 1980.

In selecting manuscript collections to be included in this guide, we considered the potential research value of each group of papers in our holdings. In evaluating small collections of ten items or less, we looked for significant correspondence. We did not include collections composed only of documents like diplomas, military orders, deeds, etc. These are readily accessible, however, through in-house finding aids.

Each descriptive overview includes a brief biographical outline derived from various sources—*The Handbook of Texas, Southwestern Historical Quarterly*, newspaper obituaries, vertical file material, and the papers themselves—and a description of the materials included in the collection.

We extend our thanks to all those who contributed to this guide; to NHPRC and H. Kempner, unincorporated, for funding projects to process nearly one thousand linear shelf feet of manuscript material; to personnel who have worked on those projects, including present staff members Van Ferguson of the Rare Books Department, Murray Allen Smith of the Kempner project, and Julia Dunn of the Archives Department; to former archivist Larry Wygant, who wrote the first NHPRC proposal; and especially to the board of directors of the library and librarian John Hyatt, who have supported the Rosenberg Library in its role as manuscripts repository. Finally, we owe an immediate debt of gratitude to the Friends of the Rosenberg Library, who have funded the publication of this guide.

Donors

THE Rosenberg Library manuscript holdings are the result of the generosity of many, many individuals and groups. The names that follow represent more than a century of concern for the preservation of historical manuscripts and for the continuing growth of this library. It is unfortunate that we do not have the space in this guide to include those who have given to our Texas collection other valuable materials—books, maps, photographs, architectural drawings, newspapers, pamphlets, and artifacts. The names of those donors, who number in the thousands, are available in the library.

Over the years, the Rosenberg has used several methods to record gifts, and some donations no doubt have gone unrecorded. For the most part, however, record keeping has been meticulous. We believe the following list of donors is complete; however, if there are omissions, we hope they will be brought to our attention.

The following, then, are those who have made the manuscript holdings of the Rosenberg Library the outstanding research tool that it is today. On behalf of past, present, and future historians of our great republic and state, we say, "Thank you."

A. Garland Adair
Mrs. Louis A. Adoue
The Adoue Foundation
John Adriance & Sons
Thomas Dunbar Affleck
Aglaian Study Club
A. Alford
R. P. Allen
American Guild of Organists, Galveston Chapter
American Red Cross, Galveston Chapter
American Women's Voluntary Services
Samuel E. Asbury

Grafton T. Austin
Mr. and Mrs. Valery Austin
Aziola Club
Louise Bache
Betty Ballinger
Howard Barnstone
Marguerite Barrett
Helen H. Batjer
Anna Batts
J. S. and W. F. Beers estate
John E. Beissner
Mary G. Beissner
Harry Bennett
Willie Hay Bennett estate
Charles H. Bentley

Mrs. C. L. Bercaw
Beta Study Club
George Beust
Max H. Bickler
V. J. Biron
Herbert B. Bisbey
Robert G. Bisbey
S. A. Bisbey
H. A. Black
Gai! Borden III
Mrs. James C. Borden
James A. Borup
R. D. Bowen
Annie Wood Briggs
Clay Stone Briggs
Ann Brindley
James L. Britton
Moritz Brock
Charles R. Brown
Ethel Buckley
Henry Bunting
Fred M. Burton
Margaret Sealy Burton
Cahill Cemetery Association
A. R. Campbell
Mrs. S. W. Campbell
Cohn Cannady
Emile Carbonnel
John E. Carter
Centre on the Strand
Marie Louise Chataignon
Edmund R. Cheeseborough
Alice Cherry
Ida May Cherry
Mildred Cherry
Ray Christensen
Frank Manning Chubb
Albert Irving Clark
Mary M. Clayton
Nicholas J. Clayton, Jr.
Isaac Monroe Cline
Coastal Fisheries
Rabbi Henry Cohen
Robert I. Cohen, Jr.
Mr. and Mrs. Nicholas Colombo

Carolyn Corn
Nellie Morgan Craig
Sarah Hawley Creson
James Crisp
The Reverend George L. Crocket
D. L. Crook
Henrietta Austin Cunningham
Robert Harriss Dalehite
Jesse Jay Dalehite, Jr.
Albert Mills Darragh
Mrs. H. W. Darst
Margaret S. Dart
Waters S. Davis
Charles L. Dealey
George B. Dealey
Ethel Degner
Charles G. Dibrell, Jr.
Dr. Alexander Dienst
Joseph W. Doby
C. E. Doherty
Sarah Doherty
Dorothy Dow
A. Stanley Dreyfus
Mrs. James H. Durgin
Dr. Joseph O. Dyer
Thomas H. Edgar
Robert C. Ehlert
Mrs. M. E. Eisenhour
L. C. Elbert
Emily Erdmann
Fred W. Erhard
Peter Erhard
George S. Ewalt
Stanley Faye
Lloyd R. Fayling, Jr.
J. M. Fendley
Sarah Ferrier
Albernese Fields
First Baptist Church, Galveston
First Hutchings–Sealy National Bank
First Lutheran Church, Galveston
First Presbyterian Church, Galveston
T. E. Flick

John W. Focke
Sherman A. Fontaine
Charles Fowler
Milo Pitcher Fox estate
Mattie Franklin
French Benevolent Society
Mrs. O. L. Fuller
Henry Fundling, Jr.
Mrs. C. E. Galloway
City of Galveston
Galveston Art League
Galveston Arts Center
Galveston Chamber of Commerce
Galveston Children's Home
Galveston Cotton Exchange and
    Board of Trade
Galveston Daily News
Galveston Garden Club
Galveston Historical Foundation
Galveston Historical Society
Galveston League of Women Voters
Galveston Little Theatre Board
Galveston Musical Club
Galveston Public Health Nursing
    Service
Mrs. J. A. Gannaway
Herbert L. Ganter
John C. Garner
Peter Gengler Company
Grace T. Gill
Girls' Literary Club
Goals for Galveston
Josephine Goldman
S. Goldman
W. W. Graves
Phyllis Green
Irene Grisaffi
George W. Grover
Walter E. Grover
Gulf, Colorado & Santa Fe Railway
George Graham Hall
Mary Seaborne Hallmark
John Tod Hamner
Rosa Tod Hamner
Mr. and Mrs. John Hanna

Parker Hanna
Mrs. A. W. Harris
Ed J. Harris
John W. Harris
Mrs. A. E. Hart
Fred Hartel
Eugene A. Hawkins
Wallace Hawkins
Matt Hemingway, Jr.
Maud Hershberger
H. P. Hervey
Captain Emil Hoby
Mrs. George Hodson
Rebecca Bell Hodson
Percy W. Holt
Charles A. Holt, Jr.
John W. Hopkins
Marian F. Houghton
Owen Howard
Hobart Hudson
James T. Huffmaster
R. W. Humphreys
Mrs. D. G. Hunt
Robert K. Hutchings
Sealy Hutchings
C. J. H. Illies estate
J. R. Irion
W. A. James
Mrs. C. L. Jenkins
Julius Jockusch
Franck C. Johnson
Mrs. Robert V. Johnson
Edward Jones
Henry J. Jumonville
Julius Kauffman
Daniel Webster Kempner
H. Kempner, unincorporated
Harris L. Kempner
I. H. Kempner
Ruth Levy Kempner
Mamie Kenefick
KGBC radio
Luther G. Knebel
Mrs. David W. Knepper
Mrs. Robert Knox

Mrs. Moritz Kopperl
Emilie B. Labadie
F. J. Lackey
John Lafitte
Mrs. and Mrs. Morris N. Lancaster
Mrs. Henry A. Landes
Lasker Home for Children
Mrs. W. Lawes
J. C. League estate
Mary D. League
Thomas Jefferson League estate
League of Women Voters
Byrd Estelle LeCompte
Mrs. Kelly Leonard
St. Clair Leonard
Joseph Levy
Marian Levy
Mary E. Liberato
Elbridge Gerry Littlejohn
John W. Lockhart
Judge William B. Lockhart
Mrs. William B. Lockhart
Lockhart, Hughes & Lockhart
Addie Love
John F. Lubben
W. G. Lyons
Samuel J. Maas
Mrs. P. S. McCaleb
Mr. and Mrs. John W. McCullough
David McCurrach, Jr.
Mrs. M. E. McFarland
D. J. McGregor
Mrs. H. R. McManus
C. H. McMaster
Captain David B. McMichael
Mrs. C. G. Magee
George E. Mann
Marie Marburger estate
Mrs. T. C. Mather
Joseph I. Maurer
Edward E. Maynard
W. Kendall Menard
Mrs. Ben Milam
Mrs. A. G. Mills
Ballinger Mills

Ballinger Mills, Jr.
Dorothy Mirror
O. D. Moody
William L. Moody III
The Moody Foundation
Mrs. George D. Morgan
James M. Morgan
Leon A. Morgan
William M. Morgan
Suzanne Morris
National Maritime Research Center
P. J. Naughton
Robert Nesbitt
H. L. Newton
Niigata Sister City Committee
Judge James L. Noel, Jr.
Thomas H. Nolan
Mary Moody Northen
Mrs. D. T. Oliver
John Olson
Greta Oppe
Mrs. W. H. Owen
J. Pabst
The Reverend Judson B. Palmer
Frank A. Park
William J. Park
Frank C. Patten
Samuel M. Penland
Mrs. D. W. Phillips
Thomas Phillips
Ella M. Plant
Mrs. O. H. Plant
Mrs. O. M. Plant
Port of Galveston
Mrs. W. B. Potter
William Quick
Silas B. Ragsdale
Dr. Edward Randall
Frances Grover Rayburn
James Rayburn
Mrs. W. L. Redman
Gene B. Reid
A. J. Ressel
John Reymershoffer

Ann Rice
Thomas G. Rice
Dr. Norman Hurd Ricker
W. R. Roberts
Henry Rosenberg
Letitia Rosenberg Women's Home
Mollie Macgill Rosenberg
Rotary Club of Galveston
Mrs. Rosa Senechal Rothsprack
Mart H. Royston
Mrs. W. C. Ruenbuhl
Henry J. Runge
Henry J. Runge, Jr.
Peter C. Rushton
Alexander Russell
Kincy Rygaard
Dr. Albert N. Sarwold
Mrs. H. Grady Saunders
Lillian Schadt
Cecil Nichols Mansfield Schelling
Joseph L. Schlankey
Albert W. Schneider
A. R. Schwartz
George Sealy, Jr.
Sealy & Smith Foundation
Elizabeth S. Sears
John Shackelford, Sr.
John Shackelford, Jr.
Mrs. R. M. Sias
Mrs. John W. Simmins
Lawrence M. Simons
William Simpson
Mrs. H. B. Sinclair
John P. Sjolander
Mrs. R. D. Smith
Mrs. James Sorley
Southern Cotton Press & Manufacturing Company
South Texas National Bank
Ernest Stavenhagen
Francis F. Steers
Beverly Walden Stein
Maco Stewart
Thomas W. Streeter
Ben C. Stuart

Theodore B. Stubbs
Sara Ellen Stubbs
Kate C. Sturgis
Dr. Howard G. Swann
Chauncey G. Sweet
Sarah Napp Tacquard
Latane Temple
Judge J. W. Terry
R. M. Tevis, Sr.
Texas Historical Society
Texas Historical Society of Galveston
Dr. and Mrs. Edward Randall Thompson
Libbie Moody Thompson
Lucy F. Thompson
Daniel K. Thorne
Mary Tod
E. A. Toebelman
Richard W. Toebelman
H. H. Treaccar
Henry M. Trueheart estate
Lella Trueheart
Mary Cecelia Tucker estate
Philip C. Tucker estate
Philip C. Tucker III
Drexel Turner
Estelle Brown Turner
Laure Underwood
United Daughters of the Confederacy, Magruder Chapter, Veuve Jefferson Davis Chapter
United States National Bank
University of Houston M. D. Anderson Library
Lee J. Valentine
J. S. Vedder
Patricia Rayburn Waldner
Mrs. W. B. Wallis
Kotaro Watanabe
Julia Webster
Mrs. Edward Wechsler
Wednesday Club
W. K. Wellborn
Rosella Horowitz Werlin

William V. Westerlage
Zebulon Lewis White, Jr.
Henry Wilkens
Marjorie A. Williams
Sally Trueheart Williams
Willie D. Williams
Theodore O. Wilson
E. W. Winkler
John M. Winterbotham

Charles Wolston
Clinton M. Wolston
Mrs. O. B. Wolston
Women's Civic League
Ralph Woods
Mr. and Mrs. George N. Yard
Young Women's Christian Association

Manuscript Sources in the Rosenberg Library

04–0001—04–0007
Huffmaster, James Taylor
Papers, 1814–50; 7 items; MS, printed.

James Taylor Huffmaster (1842–1931) settled in Galveston shortly after the end of the Civil War. A poet, hymnist, civic leader, and Methodist minister, he was for many years employed by Hutchings, Sealy & Company.

Papers are correspondence, a military commission, invitations, a social card, and an 1814 diary kept by Joseph Huffmaster, great-grandfather of James.

04–0013
Jack, William Houston
Note, 1831; 1 page; MS.

Request to Stephen F. Austin to pay bearer James Whitesides amount due. Dated June 29, 1831, in San Felipe de Austin. Receipt of Whitesides and Jack on verso.

04–0015
United States Bureau of Refugees, Freedmen, and Abandoned Lands
Records, 1865–68; 2½ inches; printed.

This collection contains printed records including general orders, circulars, and incomplete rosters of officers and civilians on duty.

04–0021
Menard, Pierre J.
Receipt, 1816; 1 page; MS.

Receipt for deerskins dated April 3, 1816, by Pierre J. Menard, fur trader in St. Genevieve, Missouri.

04–0028
Focke, John
Papers, 1861–1917; 22 items; MS, printed.

John Focke (1836–1907) was born in Oslebhausen, Germany. During the 1850s he worked in Matamoros, Mexico, for De Jersy

& Company, a cotton firm headquartered in Liverpool. Focke married Georgiana Dorothea Marckmann of La Grange, Texas, in Berlin in 1866. He settled in Galveston after the war and formed a partnership with Henry Wilkins in 1867. In 1882, H. C. Lange joined the business, and the name became Focke, Wilkins, & Lange. This name survived until 1917, when it was shortened to Wilkins & Lange.

Papers include Confederate Texas treasury warrants and script, receipts and stock certificates, a passport, a Garten Verein certificate, an incorporation notice, a promissory note, business cards, clippings, announcements, and notices of the Relief Committee following the Galveston hurricane of 1900.

04–0044
Grant, Ulysses Simpson
Letter, 1863; 1 item; MS.

Letter of March 8, 1863, to Lt. Col. G. F. Allen regarding leave-of-absence ruling for officers.

04–0049—04–0050
Roberts, Oran Milo
Letters, 1882; 2 items; MS.

Two letters from Oran Milo Roberts (1815–98), governor of Texas, to Col. J. M. Burroughs, president of Galveston Wharf Company. Letters discuss Prairie View Colored Normal School and Texas politics.

04–0066
Sherwood, Lorenzo
Scrapbook, 1851–55; 1 volume; printed.

Clippings concern the campaign of Lorenzo Sherwood for the state legislature, with discussions of the state system of internal improvements, state debt, taxation, and railroads.

06–0005
Preston & Robira
Booklet, ca. 1875; 1 item; printed.

Physician's Dose List of Elegant Preparations; Fluid Extracts, Etc., prepared and sold by Preston & Robira, druggists of Galveston.

10–0001
Dashiell, Jeremiah Yellott
Papers, 1862; 1 volume; letterpress.

Jeremiah Dashiell (1804–88) was a physician, a Mexican War veteran, inspector general of Texas during the Civil War, and editor of the *San Antonio Herald*.

Papers are correspondence dealing with Texas state troops and civil and military authorities, August 13–December 4, 1862.

14–0030
Howard Association of Galveston
Records, 1854–82; 34 items and 2 volumes; MS, printed.

The Howard Association provided nursing care and welfare for victims of yellow fever. Members were men who had once had the disease and were thought to be immune to it.

Holdings include financial records, minutes, bills, reports, correspondence, receipts, and a printed death list of the 1858 epidemic in Galveston.

15–0001
Bache, Louise F.
Report, 1915; 5 leaves; MS.

Manuscript report by Louise F. Bache, Rosenberg Library children's librarian, on the chaos in the library during the hurricane of 1915.

19–0027
American Red Cross, Galveston Chapter
Records, 1916–65; 5 feet, 2½ inches + 2 volumes; MS,
typescript, printed.

A major portion of the records of the Galveston chapter of the American Red Cross dates from World War I. Papers include correspondence, bulletins, and directives from the Red Cross southwestern office, St. Louis; shipping invoices for relief goods; list of local members and committee chairmen; financial reports listing donations and expenses; correspondence concerning awards; monthly reports; annual reports; and board minutes of Community Council of Galveston, United Fund, and Family Service Board.

22–0009—22–0021
Labadie, Nicholas Descomps
Papers, 1829–67; 1 inch; MS.

Nicholas Labadie (1801–67) was a physician and druggist in Galveston and Anahuac.

Papers include correspondence with nephew Anthony Lagrave, letters between daughters Sarah and Mary Cecelia, marriage certificates, and a cholera remedy.

22–0023
Trueheart, Henry Martyn
Family papers, 1840–1904; 7½ inches; MS, printed, typescript.

Correspondence, official papers, and transcriptions of letters pertain to family affairs and the real estate business of the H. M. Trueheart family. See also 78–0012, 78–0013, and 78–0014.

22–0024
Cheeseborough, Edmund Reed
Papers, 1902–58; 15 inches; MS, letterpress, typescript, printed.

Edmund Reed Cheeseborough was a postmaster of Galveston, secretary-treasurer of Leon & H. Blum Land Company, secretary of the Grade-Raising Board of the City of Galveston, and a member of the East End Flats Improvement Committee.

Papers concern grade-raising activities and consist of correspondence, clippings, minutes, reports, and scrapbooks.

22–0057—22–0152
Wood, Henry Augustine
Papers, 1839–60; 95 items; MS.

Henry A. Wood was a practicing physician in Boydton and Farmville, Virginia.

Papers comprise family correspondence, promissory notes, receipts, bonds, and accounting papers of Wood's drug firm.

22–0153—22–0246
Hendley, William, & Company
Records, 1843–78; 5 inches; MS, printed.

William Hendley & Company was established in 1845 by William Hendley, his brother Captain Joseph J. Hendley, Captain John L. Sleight, and Phillip Gildersleeve. The firm operated as a shipping agent handling import and export business between Galveston and Atlantic ports. Records are business papers documenting trade with persons and firms in Galveston and the interior of Texas. Holdings include notes payable, estate papers, letters, checks, promissory notes, receipts, deeds, and invoices.

Persons and firms associated with our holdings include E. O. Patton, DeWitt C. and Jabez D. Giddings, Albert Ball, John Adriance, Sam Hardeman, Ackerman & McMillam, William Dodsworth, E. J. Hart, Tucker & League, F. W. McMahan, W. P. Ballinger, Welsh & Brother, Charles B. Redfield, and Thomas C. Bunker.

22–0247
Gresham, Walter
Papers, 1834–1905; 4 feet, 7 inches; MS, letterpress.

Born in Virginia in 1841, Walter Gresham studied law and graduated from the University of Virginia in 1863. He joined the

Confederate army and fought in northern Virginia. After the war, he moved to Galveston and began the practice of law. Elected district attorney for Brazoria and Galveston counties in 1872, he was also a stockholder, director, and attorney for the Gulf, Colorado & Santa Fe Railroad. Gresham took special interest in this road and was actively involved in selecting routes, securing rights-of-way, locating stations, and superintending the business operations of the line.

In 1887, Gresham became chairman of the committee that successfully petitioned the United States government to create a deepwater port at Galveston. He represented this city in the Texas House of Representatives from 1886 to 1891, and he was elected to Congress in 1892.

Papers contain correspondence, deeds, letterpress books, leases, contracts, estate papers, shipping receipts, and bonds.

22–0249
McKinney & Williams Company
Ledgers, 1838–45; 2 volumes; MS.

Daily ledgers of the Galveston firm of McKinney & Williams, a large commission merchant firm of the republic of Texas. The firm expanded to banking after 1842.

Information includes names of debtors and creditors, items purchased and sold, and sales prices.

23–0002—23–4503
Williams, Samuel May
Papers, 1819–64; 5 feet, 5 inches; MS, with transcriptions.

Samuel May Williams (1795–1858) was land office manager and secretary of Austin's colony, naval agent for the republic of Texas, organizer and member of the executive committee of the Galveston City Company, and partner in McKinney & Williams, commission merchants. In addition to their mercantile activities, McKinney & Williams gradually took on banking functions, which they continued after they sold the commission merchant business in 1842. At the end of 1847, the Commercial & Agricultural Bank opened with Williams as president; the institution carried on extensive state and international business until Williams' death.

Holdings consist of letters and drafts of letters, bills and receipts, promissory notes, and memoranda. Nearly half the collection pertains to the business of Austin's colony; there is also a significant portion regarding the Texas revolution and the republic of Texas. Papers after 1845 concern banking interests and financial affairs. Personal papers are integrated throughout. The Rosenberg Library published an annotated calendar of the papers in 1956. An unpublished index is also available.

23–4909—23–4919
League, Thomas Massie
Papers, 1850–52; 11 items; MS.

Thomas Massie League (1808–65) was born in Baltimore. In 1836, he moved to Houston, where he engaged in merchandising. He was a charter member of the Chamber of Commerce and was also the first postmaster in Houston. In 1842, League moved to Galveston.

Papers include correspondence of the League family.

23–4920—23–4932
League, Thomas Jefferson
Papers, 1855–63; 13 items; MS.

Thomas Jefferson League (1834–74), the son of Thomas Massie League, was married to Mary Dorothea Williams (1838–1922), daughter of Samuel May Williams. A native of Baltimore, League moved to Texas with his parents. After the Civil War he joined the legal firm of Tucker & League in Galveston.

Papers include school correspondence between League and his parents and Civil War correspondence between League and his wife.

23–4997—23–5198
League, Mary D.
Papers, 1858–93; 2½ inches; MS.

Personal and business records of Mary D. League, wife of Thomas Jefferson League.

23–5210
Coahuila and Texas, State of
Laws and Decrees, 1829–34; 2½ inches; printed.

A research collection of printed laws and decrees issued by the regional government of the Mexican state, which included Texas prior to the Texas revolution. These were with the Samuel May Williams papers. In Spanish. For English translations see 70–0098.

23–5212
Masterson, Rebecca
Poetry volume, n.d.; 1 volume; typescript.

This volume of poetry is labeled "Rebecca Masterson"; however, according to library correspondence, her mother was the poet. The poems, which were compiled in 1923, were apparently written in the latter part of the nineteenth century.

24–0007—24–0035
Wells, Clinton G.
Papers, 1863–77; 29 items; MS.

Clinton Wells (1836–85) was a partner in the firm of Wolston, Wells & Vidor, cotton factors of Galveston and Houston, and he was also president of Island City Savings Bank.
Papers pertain to Wells's service as cotton agent for the Confederate quartermaster in Houston and to his later interest in the Galveston & Eastern Texas Railway Company, chartered in 1871.

24–0068—24–0070
Davis, Waters S.
Papers, 1917–18; 3 items; typescript, printed.

Papers include an oil and gas lease and evaluations of lands near Houston, Liverpool, and League City that were owned by the estate of J. C. League.

24–0088
White, Zebulon Lewis
Papers, 1805, 1860–89; 3 feet, 9 inches; MS, printed.

Zebulon White was the eastern correspondent for the *Galveston Daily News* in the 1870s. Holdings include correspondence, clippings, calling cards, scrapbooks, printed miscellanea, and an 1805 stock certificate from the Baltimore and Frederick-Town Turnpike Road. Of special interest to Galveston are manuscript letters from Richardson, Belo & Company, publishers of the *Galveston News* and the *Dallas News* to White concerning harbor improvements; and letters from Robert B. Talfor, who surveyed for the U.S. Army Corps of Engineers in New Orleans and Galveston in 1874–75.

24–0148—24–0151
Holt, Charles A., Jr.
Papers, 1900; 4 items; MS, printed.

Three letters and a broadside concerning relief efforts following the Galveston hurricane of 1900. Charles Holt was named a special clerk of the Galveston police department by Chief of Police Edwin N. Ketchum. Papers certify the identity of Holt, direct needy persons to sources of food, and request ward chairmen to give Holt preference for interviews.

25–0001—25–0521
Borden, Gail, Jr.
Papers, 1818–97; 10 inches; MS.

A native of New York State, who came to Texas via Indiana and Mississippi, Gail Borden (1801–74) founded and published the *Telegraph and Texas Register*, 1835–37, was surveyor for Austin's colony, represented the district of Lavaca in the convention of 1833, and prepared the first topographical map of Texas. He also helped lay out the site of Houston, was first collector of the Port of Galveston under the republic, was secretary and agent for the Galveston City Company, and invented processed foods, most notably condensed milk.

Our holdings include personal correspondence, tax receipts, business records, patents on inventions, travel diaries, court papers, deeds, and estate papers.

25–0522
Houston, Sam
Letter, 1851; 2 items; MS.

Dated Huntsville, October 7, 1851, to John W. Harris of Galveston, the letter concerns a political office and comments about the gift of a dog, as well as Harris's failure to write.

25–0525—25–0552
Sherman, Sidney
Papers, 1837–70; 28 items; MS.

Sidney Sherman (1805–73), major general of the Texas militia, served as commandant of Galveston in 1861. Born in Marlborough, Massachusetts, he arrived in Texas via Boston, New York, and Cincinnati. He settled first in Harrisburg and then later in Galveston. Sherman was a merchant of cotton bagging and sheet lead, and he had interests in a sawmill, railroads, and hotels.

Papers consist of correspondence, a memorial, general orders, a report, petitions, a power of attorney, and a statement of protest.

25–0553—25–0567
Wharton, John Austin
Papers, 1862–66; 15 items; MS, printed.

John Wharton (1828–65), onetime commander of Terry's Texas Rangers, was born in Nashville and came to Galveston as a child. He attended the University of South Carolina; in 1848, he married Penelope Johnson, daughter of the governor of that state. In 1859, Wharton was elected district attorney for the First Judicial District of Texas. He entered the Confederate army as captain of Company B, Terry's Texas Rangers. Wounded at Shiloh and Murfreesboro,

Wharton also participated in the Bardstown and Chickamauga campaigns; he became major general in 1863.

Papers are correspondence, general orders, biographical sketches, and letters of introduction from the Civil War career of Wharton. Included is the 1925 correspondence of Rosenberg Library accepting donation of the papers.

25–0586
Littlejohn, Sarah Helen
Account of Hurricane of 1900; 10 pages; MS, typescript.

Eight-year-old Sarah Helen Littlejohn wrote "My Experiences in the Galveston storm, September 8, 1900," only one month after the disaster. It is a vivid account of the storm as seen from her home at 3722 Avenue o½. This essay was edited by Sara Kenamore and published in the *Texas Historian* (March, 1982).

25–0591
French Benevolent Society of Galveston
Records, 1860–1925; 1½ inches; MS.

The French Benevolent Society of Galveston was founded in 1860 and incorporated in 1871. Its purpose was to give aid and assistance to needy members.

Records consist of a notebook listing members, a copy of the 1871 charter incorporating the society, and a typescript history of the organization.

25–0592
Aziola Club
Papers, 1890–1925; 5 inches and 3 volumes; MS.

The Aziola Club was a gentlemen's literary club that was especially active in Galveston during the last of the nineteenth and the beginning of the twentieth centuries.

Holdings include a cash journal, register of visitors, membership records, minute books, correspondence, articles of incorporation and liquidation, and autographs of prominent men who were offered honorary memberships.

24–0004—26–0353
Burnet, David Gouverneur
Papers, 1788–1870; 5 inches; MS.

David G. Burnet held the offices of president, vice-president, and secretary of state in the government of the republic of Texas. Prior to his arrival in Texas, Burnet had an adventurous career. He was a volunteer in the Miranda expedition to free Venezuela from Spain; he tried and failed to establish a Louisiana trading post; and he lived among the Comanche Indians for two years.

Papers include personal and family correspondence, land tax receipts, private notebooks, and military, business, and political records.

26–0372—26–0375 and 27–0033—27–0039
Sylvester, James Austin
Papers, 1836–83; 1 inch; MS, printed.

James A. Sylvester (1807–82), one of the captors of General Antonio Lopez de Santa Anna and a veteran of the Battle of San Jacinto, was a native of Baltimore. He joined the volunteer company of Sidney Sherman in Newport, Kentucky, in 1835. After the revolution, Sylvester took part in the Somervell expedition of 1842. The following year he moved to New Orleans, where he lived until his death.

Papers include correspondence to and from family members, letters concerning the capture of Santa Anna and other Texas revolutionary activities, a military commission, newspaper clippings, and a handwritten history by Sylvester of his enlistment, appointments, and discharge in the Texas army.

26–0392
Laffite, Jean
Letter, 1819; 3 pages; MS.

Letter to General James Long, dated Galveston, July 7, 1819, discusses the cooperative effort with Long against Spain. Typescript of French and English translation is included with original letter; 3 pages each.

26–0402
Dyer, Joseph Osterman
Scrapbooks, 1920–32; 3 items; MS, printed.

Joseph O. Dyer (1856–1925) was a local historian and physician who practiced in Galveston from 1881 until his death.

Scrapbooks contain articles on early Galveston, folklore, Karankawa Indians, and folk medicine. See also 79–0017.

27–0006—27–0012
Dyer, Leon
Papers, 1833–76; 7 items; MS, printed.

Letter, certificate of citizenship, affidavits, and military commission of Leon Dyer (1807–83), son of John M. and Babette Dyer.

27–0019—27–0022
Kelley, William D.
Papers, 1864; 4 items; MS.

William D. Kelley (1825–88) served as a surgeon in the 32nd Cavalry of the Confederate army in the vicinity of Alexandria, Louisiana.

Papers include a letter, an official order, and a register of surgical cases of Dr. Kelley. See also 81–0003.

27–0041
A Visit to Galveston Island in 1818
2 pages; typescript.

Typescript of notes that Philip Crosby Tucker recorded from Randall Jones's memoirs describing the camp of Jean Laffite on Galveston Island. The Texas Historical Society of Galveston owned the original manuscript, which was destroyed in the hurricane of 1900.

27–0044—27–0699 and 27–0702
Darragh, John L.
Papers, 1839–94; 1 foot, 8 inches; MS, pictorial, graphic.

John L. Darragh (1812–92), a native of Ireland, moved to Galveston in 1839. He invested heavily in real estate, and his success in this area allowed him to assume a significant role in the affairs of the city. He became one of the first aldermen of Galveston and in 1840 was elected justice of the peace. After purchasing a controlling interest in the Galveston City Company in 1865, he was made president of the organization. He was also president of the National Bank of Texas and of the Galveston Wharf Company.

Darragh suffered a physical and mental decline in the years following the Civil War. He was declared insane in 1888, and he died in Massachusetts in 1892.

Papers include correspondence, deeds, receipts, and invoices.

27–0701
J.O.L.O. Observatory
Record Book, April 22–December 27, 1861; 1 volume; MS.

Record of military watches kept by members of J.O.L.O. in their observatory at the Hendley Building in Galveston. The meaning of "J.O.L.O." is unknown.

28–0005—28–0036
Dieckmann, Christian Frederick Andreas
Papers, 1802–68; 32 items; MS.

The collection includes business records, citizenship and masonic papers, a German army discharge, and the genealogy of Christian Dieckmann (1802–70). Also of note are the receipts for repairs for the Civil War ship *Harriet Lane*.

28–0037—28–0041
Convict Labor
Contracts, 1891–93; 5 items; MS.

Contracts awarded to Ball, Hutchings & Company by the Penitentiary Board of the State of Texas for the labor and service of sixty convicts between August 11, 1891, and July 20, 1893.

28–0047—28–0051
Slave Deeds
1862–65; 5 items; MS.

Deeds of sale for six individuals.

28–0052
Park, Mrs. S. S.
Letter, 1893; 1 item; MS.

Letter to Frank A. Park from Davilla, Milam County, Texas, April 18, 1893, concerning the role of the Park family in the "runaway scrape" in the spring of 1836.

28–0061—28–0101
Franklin, Robert Morris
Papers, 1886–1909; 41 items; MS.

Papers relate to Judge Robert Franklin's role as a member of the Galveston Seawall Committee in 1886–87. Plans and proposals submitted to the committee compose the bulk of the collection.

28–0102—28–0126
Galveston Rifles Company
Papers, 1861–68, 27 items; MS, printed.

The Galveston Rifles Company was a local militia formed in 1860. Papers include correspondence, orders, an unsigned diary, receipts, a discharge certificate, an enlistment form, and quartermaster reports including the names of several soldiers.

28–0155
Mellon, Sam W.
Journal, 1853; 1 volume; MS.

Sam W. Mellon kept this journal during an 800-mile round trip by horseback from Jasper, Texas, through northeast Texas, September 20–October 20, 1853.

28–0233
Gulf, Colorado & Santa Fe Railway Company
Records, 1875–1900; 5 inches; MS, typescript, printed.

The records of the Gulf, Colorado & Santa Fe Railway Company include financial records, contracts, land certificates, a prospectus, and correspondence between George Sealy and W. B. Strong, president of the Atchison, Topeka & Santa Fe Railway Company.

28–0293
Yard, Nahor Biggs
Papers, 1839–1900; 7½ inches; MS, printed, pictorial.

Nahor Biggs Yard (1816–89), a native of New Jersey, settled in Galveston in 1838. After serving in the army of the republic of Texas he established a partnership with J. L. Briggs to form the clothing firm Briggs & Yard. During the Civil War, Yard was a colonel in the Confederate army.

In addition to managing his clothing business, Yard was treasurer of the Galveston, Houston & Henderson Railroad, a member of the first city council of Galveston, a member of the board of education of Galveston, and for twenty years president of the Howard Association in the city.

Papers consist of personal and business correspondence, tax receipts, news clippings, and papers concerning Freemasonry. Family photographs are filed with the papers.

28–0295
Burton, Margaret Sealy
Autograph Collection, 1813–1927; 2½ inches; MS, printed, pictorial.

Margaret Sealy Burton (1876–1958) was president of the Women's Civic League of Galveston and of the John Sealy Hospital Aid Society and was active with Texas Fine Arts Association, Texas State Forest Association, Daughters of the Confederacy, Texas Poetry Society, and Girls' Musical Club of Galveston. She was widely active in Red Cross volunteer services during World War I.

Letters and other autographs are organized in alphabetical order. Also included are autographed programs, a photograph and sketch of the collector, and newspaper articles about autograph auctions and collections.

Among those persons whose letters and autographs appear in this collection are Clara Barton, Otto Von Bismarck, A. Conan Doyle, C. P. Huntington, Sam Houston, Miriam Ferguson, Oliver Wendell Holmes, Washington Irving, Andrew Jackson, and Booker T. Washington.

29–0028—29–0243
Stuart, Ben C.
Papers and Scrapbooks, 1872–1926; 30 inches and 15 volumes.

Ben C. Stuart (1847–1929) began a journalism career with the *Galveston Civilian*. He later worked for the *Galveston Daily News* as a reporter, telegraph editor, and city editor.

Papers include correspondence, manuscripts of Stuart's writings on early Galveston and Texas history, and scrapbooks containing historical articles by other authors.

29–0244
Compton Manuscript
1894; 7½ inches; MS.

Thirty-five chapters of a novel written by a Miss Compton (?–1928), resident of the Letitia Rosenberg Women's Home in Galveston.

30–0028—30–0196
Sauters, John A.
Estate Papers, 1844–78; 5 inches; MS.

Estate papers of John A. Sauters (1813–73), Texas landowner and onetime German consul. Henry Rosenberg was the executor of the estate.

30–0197
Lockhart, John W.
Papers, 1849–1918; 20 inches; MS, printed, graphic.

An Alabamian by birth, John W. Lockhart (1824–1900) moved to Washington-on-the-Brazos, Texas, in 1839. In 1843, he entered Tulane University in New Orleans; four years later, he graduated from Louisville Medical College with a degree in medicine. Lockhart returned to Texas, where he operated a large plantation and practiced medicine in Chappell Hill. There he met and married Elmina C. Wallis in 1849.

During the Civil War, Lockhart served in the Confederate army as a lieutenant and an assistant surgeon. He participated in the Battle of Galveston in January, 1863.

In their later years, Lockhart and his wife spent a great deal of time in Galveston with their children. They were in the city during the hurricane of 1900, after which they made their way back to Chappell Hill. Lockhart died there a month later.

The family of John W. Lockhart published his life and letters in 1930, under the title *Sixty Years on the Brazos*.

Papers include correspondence, diaries, financial records, travel accounts, slave deeds of sale, broadsides, muster rolls, a republic of Texas land grant, and poetry.

30–0198
Galveston Harmonic Society
Minute Book, 1866–69; 1 item; MS.

The Galveston Harmonic Society was organized in 1866. The minute book contains bylaws, a list of members, reports, and minutes of weekly society meetings.

30–0199
Galveston Lyceum
Minute Book, 1882–94; 1 volume; MS.

The minute book of the Galveston Lyceum includes lists of officers and members and minutes of the meetings.

30–0200
Galveston Harbor Improvement
Survey Journal, 1890–91; 1 volume; MS.

Journal contains surveys of Galveston Harbor and Bolivar Point, 1890–91.

30–0839
Fire Department
Notebook, 1877–78; 1 volume; MS.

The handwritten notebook lists fires and alarms answered by Galveston Hook & Ladder Company No. 1 during a two-year period. See also 32–0041.

30–0849
District Court of Galveston County
Record of jury certificates, 1842–57; 1 volume; MS.

The handwritten record book contains minutes of meetings to fortify Galveston Island and certificates issued for balances due jurors for service, 1842–57.

30–0850—30–0890
Thompson, Isham
Papers, 1837–78; 41 items; MS, printed.

Isham Thompson (1810–72) was an early settler of Preston, Texas. Born in Louisiana, he married Ellen Graves in 1837. The family owned and operated a large plantation in Matagorda County, later Wharton County. Thompson was appointed the first postmaster of Preston in 1846 and became one of the first commissioners of the new county of Wharton the same year.

Papers include slave deeds, tax forms and receipts, stock certificates, land titles, estate papers, and deeds.

30–0892
Goddard, William H.
Receipts, 1859; 4 items; MS.

Papers are receipts for bills paid by William Goddard for medicine, cut wood, blankets, and nursing for the family of John Dunn of Galveston during the yellow fever epidemic.

30–0895
Garten Verein
Records, 1907–23; 5 inches and 2 volumes; MS, printed.

Chartered "for the purpose of cultivating social entertainments and promoting social intercourse, and for the maintenance of facilities for other innocent sports," the Galveston Garten Verein operated as a nonprofit corporation from 1876 until 1923. Members purchased stock in the corporation, and at the time of founding only those of German descent could belong. During the period 1880 to 1910, many of the most prominent gentlemen of Galveston and their families were members; and the Garten Verein was the scene of the most important social functions of the city.

Holdings include charter and bylaws, programs, correspondence, list of officers and committees, membership lists, financial ledgers, receipts, and bills.

30–0896
West, Hamilton A.
Papers, 1882–1904; 2½ inches; MS, printed.

Son of a prominent Galveston physician, Hamilton A. West (1880–1931) was vice-president and director of International Creosote & Construction Company, director of the Galveston Homestead & Loan Company, director and chairman of the finance committee of the Galveston Country Club, and a member of the Galveston Artillery Company, the Elks, and the Order of Eagles.

Interested in aquatic sports, West participated in many amateur swimming and diving contests in the city and won several medals in local competitions.

Holdings include legal papers, tax receipts, guardianship papers, and a will.

30–0950
Galveston & Western Railway Company
Affidavit, 1918; 1 item; typescript.

Affidavit of Walter Gresham concerning opposition of the city of Galveston to the Galveston & Western Railway Company.

30–0956—30–0991
Beach Hotel & Seaside Improvement Company
Records, 1889–97; 1 inch, MS.

Papers comprise minutes of meetings, lists of stockholders, correspondence, bonds and coupons, and legal briefs.

30–0997
Veers, John Henry
Papers, 1871–87; 1½ inches; MS.

Papers include tax receipts and a tax abstract on property owned by John H. Veers, a Galveston druggist.

30–0998
Hirzel, Richard
Papers, 1869–83; 2½ inches; MS, printed.

Richard Hirzel was a Swiss immigrant who represented cotton-exporting concerns in New Orleans and Galveston.

Holdings comprise business, personal, and estate papers.

31–0001—31–1096 and 31–1231—31–1243
Morgan, James
Papers, 1809–81; 15 inches; MS, cartographic.

James Morgan (1786–1866) was born in Philadelphia and grew up in North Carolina. In 1830, he formed a partnership with John Reed and opened a mercantile business in Texas. Morgan was a delegate to the convention of 1832, which met at San Felipe de Austin and adopted resolutions requesting reforms from the Mexican government. In 1835, Morgan joined Lorenzo de Zavala and a group of New York financiers to encourage Texas land development.

During the Texas revolution, Morgan supplied the Texas government with ships and merchandise. As commandant of Galveston Island in 1836–37, he planned and executed the fortifications of the area. At the close of the revolution, Morgan moved to what is today known as Morgan's Point, at the mouth of the San Jacinto River. He continued to work with New York financier Samuel Swartwout to promote Texas land development. He spent his later years at his home Orange Grove, where he bred cattle, experimented with crops, and entertained well-known guests.

Holdings include personal, family, and military papers covering land speculation in Texas and the Texas revolution. Papers are letters, bills, receipts, maps, and military orders. An important group of letters between Morgan and Swartwout, dated 1836–48, was published in *Fragile Empires*, edited by Feris A. Bass, Jr., and B. R. Brunson and published by Shoal Creek (Austin, 1978).

31–1163
Galvez, Bernardo de
Land grant, 1781; 2 pages; MS.

Spanish document (August 1, 1781) granting eight patents of land at Grand Prairie, Louisiana, to Antonio Boidore. A 1931 English translation of the document by Dr. Carlos E. Castaneda accompanies the manuscript.

31–1165
McGrea, Susan E.
Letter, ca. 1880; 12 pages; MS.

The letter is an account of early days in Texas and includes a description of relations between settlers and Indians in Lampasas County, 1847–80.

31–1178
Galveston Hussar Cavalry
Papers, 1841–43; 14 pages; MS.

Papers pertain to the organization of the Galveston Hussar Company in 1841. The collection includes orders, rosters, and receipts.

31–1180—31–1183
Weiss, William and Napoleon
Letters, 1863–64; 4 items; MS.

Letters from William and Napoleon Weiss to their mother in Jasper County describe their activities in Camp Carrion Crow and Sabine, Texas, during the Civil War.

31–1191—31–1194
Davis, Edmund Jackson
Letters, 1876; 7 pages; MS, printed.

The letters from Edmund J. Davis to William P. Daran of Brenham describe incidents in Galveston during the Civil War.

32–0001
Gulf, Colorado & Santa Fe Railway Company
Authorization, 1886; 3 items; MS, typescript.

Document authorizing George Sealy to make the best possible trade in selling the Gulf, Colorado & Santa Fe Railway Company to the Atchison, Topeka & Santa Fe Railway. Papers include original and typed transcripts accompanied by a 1932 letter from Sealy explaining the significance of the document.

32–0005
Hobby, Alfred Marmaduke
Letter, 1873; 2 items; MS.

Letter from Alfred Marmaduke Hobby, president of Galveston Chamber of Commerce, to geologist S. T. Peckham of Akron, Ohio. Hobby requests information regarding a substance commonly found in Texas, which he suggests may be oil or liquid asphalt. The letter is dated September 14, 1873, twenty-eight years before the discovery of oil at Spindletop.

32–0008
Bragg, Braxton
Papers, 1849–78; 2½ inches; MS, typescript, printed.

Born in Georgia, Braxton Bragg graduated from West Point in 1837. In 1846, he went to Texas, where he fought in the Mexican War. Between the Mexican and Civil wars, he was a civil engineer in Louisiana. Bragg joined the army of the Confederacy in 1861 as a brigadier general. He became a major general at the Battle of Shiloh, and he also engaged in the Battles of Perrysville and Chattanooga. He later served as military adviser to Jefferson Davis in Richmond.

After retirement from military service, Bragg was the chief engineer of the Gulf, Colorado & Santa Fe Railway Company. In this capacity he selected the route for the line between Galveston and Brenham.

Holdings include correspondence between Bragg and his wife. Other correspondents are James H. Otey, James Duncan, Elise Brooks Ellis, Mary F. Love, Elise Hutchings, Kate Kirkham, Towson Ellis, T. O. Moore, J. L. Shriver, Samuel S. Shriver, Price Williams, J. H. Simpson, A. C. Story, Dunbar Bragg, E. B. M. Butler, Hugh L. Cole, Harry B. Sass, Albert Somerville, George B. Nicholls, Henry Rosenberg, and J. P. Fresenius.

32–0041
Galveston Hook & Ladder Company
Papers, 1867–79; 12 items; MS.

Galveston Hook & Ladder Company papers include correspondence, minutes, and a cash book. See also 30–0839.

32–0066
Texas (Steam Dredge)
Logbook, 1904; 1 volume; MS.

Logbook kept aboard the steam dredge *Texas* on a voyage from Danzig to Galveston in 1904. The dredge was to participate in the grade-raising project, but it was lost at sea on December 25, 1904.

33–0001
Moore, Edwin Ward
Letter, 1842; 3 items; typescript, photocopy.

The item is a photocopy of a letter dated August 12, 1842, to Mayor Dennis Prieur of New Orleans from Commander E. W. Moore of the Texas navy. In the letter Moore requests the extradition of ten men charged with mutiny and desertion of the Texas schooner of war *San Antonio*. Included with the letter is a typed transcript and a letter of donation to the Rosenberg Library.

33–0004—33–0012
Affleck, Thomas
Papers, 1847–66; 14 items; MS, printed.

Thomas Affleck (1812–68), a native of Scotland, established Glenblythe plantation near Brenham, Texas, in 1858. Interested in the use of scientific methods in farming, Affleck contributed to the progress of southern agriculture through the publication of his research and experimentation at Glenblythe. Two of his works, *The Cotton Plantation Record and Account Book* and *The Sugar Plantation Record and Account Book*, became models for southern planters.

An enthusiastic supporter of immigration and land development, Affleck made several trips to Great Britain to encourage potential emigrants to move to Texas. In addition, he prompted European interests to establish packing houses in Texas.

Papers include reminiscences, receipts, biographical sketches, circulars, clippings, and advertisements from Glenblythe plantation that reflect Affleck's efforts to establish the Texas Land, Labor & Immigration Company in 1866.

33–0014—33–0020
Galveston & Brazos Navigation Company
Papers, 1853–74; 7 items; MS.

Papers are from the files of Nahor Biggs Yard, onetime secretary-treasurer of the Galveston & Brazos Navigation Company. Included are a deposit book, correspondence, and records of accounts.

33–0021—33–0023
Bradbury, D.
Papers, 1861; 3 items; MS.

Correspondence between D. Bradbury and Nahor Biggs Yard concerns the resignation of General Sidney Sherman and the defense of Galveston.

33–0041—33–0093
Greenleve, Block & Company
Records, 1865–83; 52 items; MS.

Greenleve, Block & Company was a wholesale dry goods firm in Galveston. Records include correspondence, receipts, shipping lists, a ledger, and insurance policies.

33–0097
Rosenberg Family
Papers, 1837–1925; 2 feet, 8½ inches; MS.

Henry Rosenberg (1824–93) was a native of Switzerland. At the age of nineteen, he immigrated to Galveston and joined John Hessly in the dry goods business. Two years later Rosenberg bought the business from Hessly, and it grew to be one of the largest of its kind in Texas.

The role of Rosenberg in the commercial and civic life of Galveston was extensive. He organized the Galveston Bank & Trust Company, and he was a director of the First National Bank, the Galveston City Railway Company, and the Galveston Wharf Company. Rosenberg was director and president of the Gulf, Colorado & Santa Fe Railway Company, and he was Swiss consul in Galveston for many years. In 1882, he established H. Rosenberg, Banker, and he was sole owner of the bank until his death.

In addition to his business activities, Rosenberg actively supported Trinity and Grace Episcopal churches, the YMCA of Galveston, and the Galveston Orphans Home; and he served on the board of aldermen of Galveston in 1871–72 and 1885–87.

Rosenberg married twice: in 1851, to Letitia Cooper, who died June 4, 1888; and in 1889, to Mary Ragan (Mollie) Macgill, who died in 1917. He had no children.

Rosenberg died on May 12, 1893, and was buried in London Park Cemetery, Baltimore, Maryland. He bequeathed his estate to his native village of Bilten, Switzerland, and to Galveston. Some of his Galveston donations included the Letitia Rosenberg Women's Home, the YMCA building, a monument to the memory of the heroes of the Texas revolution, the Rosenberg fountains, and the Rosenberg Library.

Papers include correspondence, deeds, legal documents, business papers, ledger books, receipt books, a scrapbook, a journal, a ship's log, and papers pertaining to the benefactions of Henry and Mollie Macgill Rosenberg.

34–0003—34–0018
Seeligson, George
Papers, 1895–1911; 16 items; MS.

Papers comprise financial and business records of George Seeligson (1841–1912), Galveston wholesale merchant prominent in business and social affairs.

34–0021—34–0030
Galveston County Board of Engineers
Papers, 1902–26; 10 items; MS.

Papers include reports to the Galveston County Commissioners' Court and correspondence concerning the construction of the seawall at Galveston.

34–0033
Winterbotham, John Miller
Autograph collection, 1772–1934; 500 items; MS.

Collection comprises autographs of well-known American and British citizens.

35–0005—35–0016
Sjolander, John Peter
Papers, 1915; 12 items; MS, typescript.

Nine poems and a brief biographical sketch of John P. Sjolander compose this collection. Also included are two letters written from Sjolander to E. G. Littlejohn in 1915.

35–0018—35–0122
Littlejohn, Elbridge Gerry
Reminiscences, 1899–1935; 2½ inches; MS.

Elbridge Gerry Littlejohn (1862–1935), Galveston educator and superintendent of schools, was for thirty years secretary of the

Texas Historical Society of Galveston. In this role he persuaded many pioneers over the state to record their experiences for the society.

Events and people discussed in the letters are the Battle of Sabine Pass, Dr. Nicholas D. Labadie, Dick Dowling, Euclid M. Cox, Moses Austin, A. C. Allen, John R. Baker, Ellis P. Bean, Valentine Bennet, John B. Denton, John Durst, Sam Houston, Mirabeau B. Lamar, Dr. Gideon Lincecum, James Albert Massie, H. B. Kelsey, Thomas J. Pilgrim, Timothy Pilsbury, Philip Nolan, Thomas J. Rusk, Albert Sidney Johnston, Sidney Sherman, "Deaf" Smith, John W. Smith, Edward S. Terrell, Lorenzo de Zavala, John C. C. Hill, Dunham (Mier prisoner), Mier expedition, B. Z. Boone, "The Babe of the Alamo," Gail Borden, and the Galveston Free Library.

36–0002
Fatio, Felipe
Papers, 1817–19; 82 pages; typescript.

Typescript of correspondence of the vice-consul in New Orleans, Diego Morphy, with the captain general of the island of Cuba, 1817–19. Location of original correspondence is unknown.

36–0003—36–0009
Allen, John Melville
Papers, 1836–47; 7 items; MS, printed.

John Melville Allen (1799–1847) was the first mayor of Galveston. Born in Kentucky, he moved to Texas in 1830. In 1835, he took part in the Tampico expedition; and in 1836, he fought in the Battle of San Jacinto.

Papers consist of a letter, a contract, a muster roll of the Tampico expedition, a presidential appointment, newspaper clippings, an obituary, and a memorial.

36–0010
Galveston Mercantile Library and Galveston Free Library
Papers, 1870–78; 1 inch; MS, printed.

Established by the Galveston Chamber of Commerce in 1870, the Galveston Mercantile Library was the forerunner of the Galveston Public Library and the Rosenberg Library.

Papers are application forms, bookplates, printed rules, correspondence, receipts and statements, the ordinance and bylaws, and an insurance policy.

36–0041
Rice, Edwin E.
Journal, 1862–63; 1 volume; MS.

The journal of Sergeant Major Edwin E. Rice describes the events of 1862–63 in Major E. S. Bolling's company (First Infantry Battalion) of Waul's Legion, the army of the Confederacy.

36–0045—36–1201
Beers Family
Papers, 1777–1925; 20 inches; MS.

Personal and business papers of the Beers family headed by Jonathan S. Beers, who settled in Galveston in 1858.

Papers include letters, deeds, promissory notes, manuscript maps, a land grant, bank books, ledgers, cash books, letterpress books, scrapbooks, bills, receipts, indentures, and musical programs.

36–1202
Illies-McKenzie Family
Papers, 1800–1949; 5 inches; MS.

The Illies-McKenzie family papers reflect the activities of German immigrant John H. Illies (1813–66), who settled in Galveston in 1843; his first and second wives, Cecilia Dufour and Justine Liese; his son by Justine, Charles J. H. Illies (1862–1939); and Justine Illies's second husband, Donald McKenzie.

The papers include correspondence in English and German between the elder Illies and his successive wives, property receipts and statements, insurance policies, bank books, tax receipts, and receipts for expenses of the Galveston Art Gallery.

36–1203
Local Events
Calendar, 1928–36; 1½ inches; MS, typescript, printed.

The calendar compiled by the Rosenberg Library lists events in Galveston during the period 1928–36.

36–1205—36–1207
Galveston Port Society
Records, 1858–74; 2½ inches; MS, printed.

The records of the Galveston Port Society include ledgers, a constitution, a list of subscribers, minutes of meetings, an account book, and treasurer's reports, 1858–71. Also with the records are printed constitutions and bylaws of the Seamen's Benevolent & Life-Boat Association of Galveston and the Galveston Seamen's Home.

37–1003
Women's Civic League
Records, 1927–37; 2½ inches; MS.

Formed in 1900 as the Women's Health Protective Association, the league took the new name in 1924. Several hundred strong at the peak of membership, the league worked for the beautification of Galveston. It cooperated with the Reconstruction Finance Corporation in 1933 to manage work for the unemployed of the city and to provide food for needy persons.

Records comprise correspondence, committee notes, and notes of the corresponding secretary.

38–0001
McClellan, W. B.
Slave Deed, 186——; 1 item; typescript.

Copy of a deed of W. B. McClellan giving a slave girl to his daughter, Susan E. McCane. Dated November 24, 186——.

38–0003
Galveston Rotary Club
Records, 1913–76; 5 feet, 2½ inches; MS, printed.

The Galveston Rotary Club, which was founded in 1913, is one
of the oldest in the nation. The local organization was active during
World War I, and there is a great deal of correspondence between
the club and federal agencies concerning the war and the transfer
to a peacetime economy. Special concerns of the club were bonds
for municipal improvements, such as the grade raising, new ferry-
boats, and the Galveston-Bolivar highway; educational and recreational work among crippled children, underprivileged boys, and
orphans; and public health.

Records include correspondence, a printed constitution and
bylaws, membership rosters, pamphlets, scrapbooks, audit reports,
broadsides, minute books, and magazines.

40–0002—40–0015b
Armstrong, Thaddeus
Papers, 1849–66; 15 items; MS, printed.

The Thaddeus Armstrong papers contain correspondence, military orders, a muster roll, amnesty papers, and an account of a trip
to California in 1849.

40–0016
Branard, George A.
Diary, 1864–65; 80 pages; typescript.

The diary of George A. Branard recounts his experiences in
the Confederate army during the last year of the Civil War.

Mrs. Agnes Bushong transcribed the diary in 1940 from the
original lent by Richard Schwartz.

40–0027
Anderson, Charles Harper
Papers, 1928–40; 5 inches; MS.

Charles Harper Anderson was born in Virginia in 1875 and attended public schools there. In 1894, he moved to Galveston to

study law in the office of Scott, Levi & Smith. He was admitted to the bar in 1897. In 1901, Anderson began his long legal association with J. C. League, land speculator.

Anderson served as officer and/or director of the Citizen's State Bank of Texas City, the League City Telephone Company, the George Ball Association, United Charities of Galveston, the Rosenberg Library, Trinity Episcopal Church, and the Galveston Orphans' Home. The papers, consisting almost entirely of correspondence, pertain to Anderson's business, civic, and personal affairs.

41–0002—41–0005
McCoy, F. E.
Papers, 1844–67; 15 items; MS, typescript.

The F. E. McCoy papers contain correspondence and receipts concerning yellow fever, lynchings in Galveston, treatment of Afro-Americans, attitudes on slavery, and religious conditions in Galveston during the period 1844–67.

42–0004—42–0231
Wallis Family
Papers, 1818–1904; 228 items; MS.

John C. Wallis (1829–72), born in Alabama, moved to Chappell Hill, Texas, in 1848. After serving in the army of the Confederacy, he moved to Galveston and established the firm of Wallis, Landes & Company, wholesale grocers and cotton factors. Wallis was a founder of the Texas Banking & Insurance Company and president of the Galveston Chamber of Commerce.

Joseph Wallis, the brother of John, was an officer of the Galveston & Western Railway, the Gulf City Compress Company, and the Texas Guarantee & Trust Company. From 1872 until his death in 1907, Joseph was the senior partner of Wallis, Landes & Company.

Papers include personal letters from family members in Alabama, North Carolina, Mississippi, and Texas and business letters regarding cotton sales from the family plantation at Chappell Hill. Also present is a cash journal of J. E. Wallis dated 1861–65, recording Confederate war tax payments, business loans and payments, information on cotton crops and sales, and payments to freedmen. Other materials are enlistment registers of Washington County men entering the Confederate army and letters from J. E. Wallis to his wife Kate while he was stationed at forts in the Galveston area. Later papers are contracts between the Wallis family and former slaves and business papers of Wallis, Landes & Company.

42–0232—42–0287
Bennett, Harry
Papers, 1917–42; 56 items; MS.

Harry Bennett (1892–1942) was a merchant seaman and rare book collector who designated the Rosenberg Library as his sole beneficiary. His papers include correspondence, receipts, photographs, and insurance cards.

44–0001
Seargent, Thomas
Letter, 1867; 1 item; MS.

Letter of Thomas Seargent of Galveston to his sister Annie E. Seargent of Stanford, Kentucky. Seargent describes crop conditions, the yellow fever epidemic, and banking conditions.

44–0002—44–0005
Hitchcock & Company
Papers, 1856; 4 items; MS.

Correspondence concerns the sale of six condemned iron guns to Hitchcock & Company for export to China. Authorization is signed by Jefferson Davis.

44–0006
Thames, R. I.
Slave deed, 1850; 1 item; MS.

Deed of sale for slaves sold by Charles Alexander of Louisiana to R. I. Thames, March 23, 1850.

44–0007
Grosse-Tête Flying Artillery
Report, 1864; 2 items; MS.

Description and report of armaments of the Grosse-Tête Flying
Artillery, June 17, 1864.

44–0008—44–0015
Confederate States of America
Military orders, 1861–62; 8 items; MS.

Orders issued from the Galveston headquarters. Transcripts are
included with the orders.

44–0016
Sealy, George
Letter, 1898; 1 item; MS.

The letter from Collis P. Huntington to George Seely (*sic*) concerns the possible extension of the Southern Pacific Railroad to Galveston.

44–0019
Collins, Joseph
Letter, 1806; 1 item; MS.

The letter to Vicente Sebastin Pintado of Pensacola, from Joseph Collins of Paskagula (*sic*), concerns land matters.

46–0002
Galveston City Company
Papers, 1834–1962; 15 inches; MS, typescript, photostat,
cartographic.

Michel B. Menard, Thomas F. McKinney, Samuel May Williams, and J. K. Allen were the leading stockholders in the Galveston City Company, which was incorporated according to an act of the congress of the republic of Texas in 1841. The company had the authority to survey and sell lots and to do early city planning. The corporation was dissolved in 1944.

This is an artificial collection composed of items and sets of papers donated to the Rosenberg Library over a period of seventy years. Holdings include stock certificates, reports of company agents, balance sheets showing property holdings, petitions, authorizations and memoranda concerning requests for land, and correspondence between company officers and agents. Records of the 1898 Sealy-Huntington proposal for a Southern Pacific terminal in Galveston are of note, as are those of suits brought against the company by the state and federal governments over the ownership of east end of Galveston Island.

46–0006
Blagden, John D.
Letter, 1900; 7 pages; MS.

John D. Blagden was on temporary assignment with the Galveston Weather Bureau in September, 1900. His letter to a family in Duluth describes the disastrous hurricane of that year.

47–0001
Chauldron, Jean Simon
Letters, 1817–18; 5 items; typescript.

Transcript copies of unsigned letters from the province of Texas to Philadelphian Jean Simon Chauldron, publisher of the first French newspaper in the United States.

47–0002
"Champ d'Asile"
Article, 1818; 7 pages; typescript.

Originally published in *L'Abeille Americaine* on July 9, 1818, "Champ d'Asile" describes the French colony in the province of Texas.

47–0003—47–0028
Bunting, Robert F.
Papers, 1874–80; 1½ inches; MS, typescript, printed.

Papers include patent specifications, diagrams, contracts, deeds, and correspondence pertaining to Marcusy's Floating Docks.

47–0029—47–0031
Laffite Family
Records, 1767–1895; 3 items; photostat.

Records from Laffite-Mortimore family Bible. The authenticity of these records is in question.

48–0007—48–0010
Maas, Samuel
Papers, 1800–97; 4 items; MS.

The Samuel Maas papers contain charter party agreements with George W. Lothrop, owner of the schooner *Alert*, for a voyage from Charleston to Galveston; an inventory dated July 10, 1800, of the estate of Robert Lambert of Pittsburgh; and a receipt and shipping voucher for goods shipped on the schooner *Burleson*.

48–0050
Jones, Levi
Deposition, 1868; 19 pages; MS.

Deposition made by Levi Jones for *City of Galveston* v. *Galveston Wharf & Cotton Press Company*. Interrogatories are attached.

48–0080
Women's Choral Club of Galveston
Records, 1923–25; 1 volume; MS.

Record book contains the constitution, lists of members, minutes, and correspondence of the Women's Choral Club of Galveston.

48–0103
Watson, Nellie
Letter, 1915; 9 leaves; typescript.

Letter from nurse Nellie Watson to "Billy." In the nine-page document Watson describes her experiences during the hurricane of 1915.

49–0001—49–0006
Ball, Hutchings & Company
Records, 1885–94; 6 items; MS.

Partnership papers of the Ball, Hutchings & Company bankers. Principals include John H. Hutchings, George Sealy, Rebecca Sealy, and Sarah Ball. See also 80–0001.

49–0007—49–0013
Lynn, Arthur Thomas
Papers, 1846–50; 7 items; MS.

Papers include official documents pertaining to Lynn's service as British consul at Galveston. President Zachary Taylor's acknowledgment of the appointment is among the documents.

49–0014—49–0021
Stowe, William N., Jr.
Papers, 1868–1950; 8 items; MS, typescript, printed.

Papers include a bill for goods on the steamer *Mustang*, theater and ball programs, a pass issued to Stowe following the 1900 hurricane, and a letter from Stowe telling of his experience in the cleanup after the storm.

50–0001
Ballinger, William Pitt
Papers, 1832–1947; 3 feet, 9 inches; MS, printed.

William Pitt Ballinger (1825–88), born in Kentucky, came to Galveston in 1843 to study law with his uncle James Love. When the Mexican War began, he volunteered for service and rose from private to adjutant in Albert Sidney Johnston's regiment. In 1850, Ballinger was appointed United States district attorney for the Texas district; in 1854, he resigned to enter private practice in Galveston.

During the Civil War, Ballinger was one of a committee sent to Richmond to obtain defensive armaments for Galveston, and he served as Confederate receiver in the city for the duration of the war. Toward the end of the war, Ballinger went to New Orleans to negotiate the surrender of Texas and to try to prevent the occupation of the state by the Union army.

Ballinger twice declined appointment to the Supreme Court of Texas, but he was a member of the judicial committee in the constitutional convention of 1875. He died in Galveston.

Papers include diaries (1854–68, 1871–87), correspondence, writings, and clippings. The University of Texas has copies of the diaries, which they have indexed.

50–0307
Grover, Walter
Article, 1950; one item; typescript.

This article is an illustrated historical sketch (1836–1936) of Galveston Island west of the city limits of 1950.

50–0415
Mier Expedition
Prisoners' list, 1844; 20 leaves; MS, typescript.

List of prisoners of the Mier expedition, compiled by Henry Journey, September 13, 1844.

50–0437
Gray, Millie
Diary, 1832–40; 1 volume; MS.

Diary recording experiences of Millie Gray of Fredericksburg, Virginia. Included with the diary is Gray's "small journal," in which she describes events on her journey to Texas in 1838. The diary was published by Fletcher Young for the Rosenberg Library Press in 1967.

51–0004—51–0125
Grover, George W.
Papers, 1824–1901; 5 inches; MS.

George W. Grover (1819–1901) was born in New York and moved to Texas in 1839 or 1840. In 1841, he joined the Santa Fe expedition and was captured and imprisoned near Mexico City. While in prison he edited the *True Blue*, a manuscript newspaper that survives in this collection. After his release from the Mexican prison, Grover joined the argonauts in California. He returned to Texas in 1850 and entered business in Galveston. During the Civil War he served as alderman and was mayor of Galveston for a short time. During his later years he was active in the Galveston County Veterans Association and the Galveston Historical Society.

Papers include correspondence pertaining to the Galveston City Company, Grover's diary of the Santa Fe expedition, handwritten editions of *True Blue*, poetry, a letter describing travel from Galveston to Cincinnati in 1851, a slave deed of sale, tax receipts, a sketch of vessels blockading Galveston (1864), minutes and correspondence of the Galveston County Veterans Association (1874–90), a Galveston Public Library poster (1884), text of a speech and several articles presented to the Galveston Historical Society (1895–1900), and scrapbooks containing clippings, articles, poetry, and Grover's account of the Galveston hurricane of 1900.

51–0126
United Daughters of the Confederacy, Veuve Jefferson Davis Chapter No. 17
Records, 1901–51; 5 inches; MS, printed.

Organized in 1895, Chapter No. 17 of the Texas Division of United Daughters of the Confederacy remains active into the 1980s. Papers include membership applications, membership certificates, a constitution, bylaws, a catechism, and minute books.

52–0019—52–0023
Hutchings, Sealy & Company
Papers, 1897–1927; 5 items; MS.

Papers include a letter dated September 13, 1898, to George Sealy from John Sealy discussing the sale of a cotton compress to Kempner interests and a strike of black workers on the Mallory dock; an announcement regarding the name change of the Galveston bank from Ball, Hutchings & Company to Hutchings, Sealy & Company; and a document assigning the power of attorney of John Sealy to George Sealy.

52–0030—52–0121
Galveston City Sexton
Records, 1847–51; 88 items; MS.

Scattered burial records reported by city sexton John Griffin.

52–0122
Eaton, Benjamin
Papers, 1839–97; 2½ inches; MS, photostat.

Born in Dublin, Ireland, ca. 1805, Benjamin Eaton attended Trinity College. He entered the Episcopal priesthood in 1839 and became a missionary in America. After serving briefly in Wisconsin, he went to Texas in 1840. Eaton served as rector of Trinity Church, Galveston, from 1841 until his death in 1871.

Papers include correspondence, deeds, bills of sale, stock certificates, promissory notes, loan agreements, and land grants.

52–0123
Galveston Art League
Records, 1914–46; 7½ inches; MS, printed.

The Galveston Art League was founded in 1914 by a group composed of Mrs. Boyer Gonzales, Frances Kirk, Hattie Wittig, Mrs. I. H. Kempner, Angela McDonald, Mrs. W. F. Beers, and Alice Block. The constitution of the league states that it will "foster worth-while art in the schools and homes of the city, solicit the cooperation of public and private groups in the support of art, encourage the artists of the city and state, and hold exhibitions." The permanent collection of the league is housed in the Rosenberg Library.

Papers include correspondence, clippings, programs, minutes, treasury reports, annual reports, and membership lists.

53–0001
Royal Yacht (Schooner)
Logbook, 1862–63; 1 item; MS.

Captain Thomas H. Chubb's log of the Confederate schooner *Royal Yacht*, May 27, 1862–January 1, 1863.

55–0001
Underwood, Joe P.
Diary, 1864–65; 45 pages; photostat.

Transcript of the diary of Joe P. Underwood, a member of Gibson's battery, Squire Battalion, General Forney's division, light artillery, Texas infantry. Underwood was stationed at Camp Magruder near Minden, Louisiana, in 1864–65.

55–0004
Galveston Harbor
Scrapbook, 1951–55; 1 volume; typescript, printed, pictorial.

Scrapbook titled "History of Galveston Harbor" compiled by Walter E. Grover.

56–0005
Kauffman & Runge
Records, 1848–1956; 8 feet, 9 inches and 21 volumes; MS, printed.

The partnership of Kauffman & Runge, commission merchants, was the successor firm to Julius Kauffman & Company, which was established in 1842.

Henry Runge (1816–73), a German immigrant, joined Kauffman in 1868; under their leadership the firm became the largest cotton-exporting house in Galveston after the Civil War.

Holdings include ledgers and correspondence of the firm under both names. A major part of this correspondence is that of Henry J. Runge (1859–1922), the son of the elder Runge. This material documents the interest of the son in land speculation, an outgrowth of the commission merchant business.

Also included are correspondence and financial papers of the Galveston Land & Improvement Company. Julius Runge (1851–1906), cousin of Henry J. Runge, was vice-president of this company, which developed the Denver Resurvey in Galveston in the early 1890s.

Later correspondence is of Henry J. Runge, Jr. (1887–1956), son of Julius. The younger man represented A. M. Lockett Company as a machinery and contracting engineer. He was active in the Galveston Rotary Club and the Galveston Chamber of Commerce.

60–0002
Meyer Family
Papers, 1839–40; 17 items; MS.

Papers include a birth certificate, letter, bills, and receipts of the Ludwig Meyer family.

62–0001
Houston, Sam
Bank draft, December 14, 1825; 1 item; MS.

Draft on the Branch Bank of the United States in Washington, D.C. Houston was a United States congressman from Tennessee at the time.

62–0003—62–0200 and 62–0202
Rice, Thomas Geale
Papers and scrapbook, 1942–58; 197 items and 1 volume; MS, typescript, printed.

Papers of Thomas Geale Rice (1905–62), journalist and local historian. Included are correspondence, news clippings, literary productions, and historical notes.

62–0201

Red Cross, Galveston Chapter

Report, 1962; 1½ inches; typescript.

Report of the Galveston County Chapter of the American Red Cross on disaster operations during the emergency phase of hurricane Carla. Report is dated February 1, 1962.

63–0002

Harris, Pryor Nance

Journal, 1880–81; 1 item; MS.

Notebook containing information on businesses and businessmen in Texas in 1880.

65–0002

KGBC, Hurricane Carla

Records, 1961–64; 2½ inches; MS, typescript, printed.

Records include transcripts of KGBC radio announcements during hurricane Carla; records from various agencies describing the event and its aftermath; and correspondence from KGBC listeners who were grateful for the station's information during the storm.

Included is correspondence to Steve Cowan, general manager of KGBC, from I. H. Kempner, Galveston County Judge Peter J. LaValle, Texas Attorney General Will Wilson, and citizens of the city of Galveston and surrounding area.

65–0003

Cox, Catherine Isabella

Life sketch, 1901; 20 pages; typescript.

Biographical sketch of Catherine Isabella Cox, wife of General Sidney Sherman. Cox's daughter, Belle Sherman Kendall, wrote the essay.

65–0008

Walker, Mamie Ketchum

Letter, 1965; 1 page; typescript.

Letter to Virginia Eisenhour from Mamie Ketchum Walker discussing the history of the Michel B. Menard residence in Galveston.

65–0009
Harris, Annie Pleasants
Memoirs, 1823–39; 8 leaves; typescript.

Transcript of the memoirs of Annie P. Harris, who was an early settler in Texas. Papers include the correspondence between the Rosenberg Library and donor John W. Harris, grandson of the author.

66–0001—66–0015
Republic of Texas, State of Texas
Treasury warrants and certificates, 1837–61; 15 items; MS.

Treasury warrants for salaries of the judiciary, attorney general, and other employees; relief for Texas citizens held prisoner in Mexico; and protection from enemy Indian tribes. Collection also includes Texas state certificates of payment for debts incurred by the republic of Texas.

66–0042
Mardi Gras
Materials, 1867–1966; 7½ inches; printed.

The Mardi Gras in Galveston was a city-wide event from 1867 until the early 1950s and included masqued balls, parades, receptions, and general revelry. Although only a small portion of the citizenry received invitations to the balls, everyone joined in the parades and carnival atmosphere.

Materials are programs, invitations, and news clippings.

67–0021—67–0022
Girls' Literary Club of Galveston
Records, 1915–17; 2 volumes; MS.

Records of the Girls' Literary Club, which was sponsored by the Rosenberg Library Children's Department. Louise Bache was the children's librarian.

67–0080
Wilson, Theodore O.
Papers, 1849–72; 2½ inches; MS.

Personal correspondence and some business papers of Theodore O. Wilson, a clothier in Galveston.

Papers are correspondence, receipts, bills and accounts, an insurance policy, deeds, court documents, and an indenture.

68–0039 and 68–0057—68–0074
Nolan, Thomas H.
Papers, 1902; 19 items; MS.

Series of letters to the Honorable Thomas H. Nolan of Galveston in support of state aid for the city following the hurricane of 1900.

68–0143—68–0147
City Engineer of Galveston
Letters, 1900–1901; 5 items; MS, typescript.

Letters written to the office of the city engineer after the hurricane of 1900. Subjects include missing persons, inquiries about job opportunities, plans for hiring clean-up crews, and needs of the fire department.

68–0158
Grover, Walter E.
Article, 1963; 13 pages; typescript.

Typescript of the memoirs of Walter E. Grover (1869–1960) describing life in Galveston during the late nineteenth century; from the files of Kincy Rygaard.

69–0005—69–0050
Dobbins, Archibald S.
Papers, 1852–69; 46 items; MS, typescript, printed.

The papers comprise correspondence, a will, legal papers, army documents, clippings, photographs, and a life sketch of southern planter Archibald S. Dobbins (ca. 1827–70). During the Civil War, Dobbins was commander of Dobbins' First Arkansas Cavalry Brigade, C.S.A. After the war he moved to New Orleans, where he established the firm Dobbins, Pleasants & Company, commission merchants. In 1867, he moved to Brazil and settled on the Amazon River in the city of Santarem.

69–0243
Priestly, William
Letter, October 31, 1944; 14 pages; typescript.

Letter dated October 31, 1944, to Clare Boothe Luce from William Priestly, in which he discusses his experiences in a Japanese prison camp.

69–0247—69–0263
Thompson, James Edwin
Papers, 1858–1965; 17 items; MS, typescript, printed.

Stock certificates, invitations, speeches, and court records of James E. Thompson (1863–1927), a Galveston physician and professor of medicine at the University of Texas Medical Branch.

69–0266—69–0273
Sampson, Henry
Papers, 1871; 8 items; MS.

Incoming correspondence pertaining to investments of Henry Sampson. See also 72–0524—72–1992.

69–0274
Gautier Family
Papers, 1819–1930; 2½ inches; MS.

Personal papers and some business records of Pierre Gautier and his son Achille. The elder Gautier was a confectioner and liquor dealer in Mexico City, Tampico, and Matamoros, Mexico. Achille Gautier (1845–1924) moved the family business to Galveston in 1865.

Papers are correspondence, bills, receipts, memoranda, exchange notes, consignment certificates, news clippings, an instrument of protest, and a slave deed of sale.

69–0275
Kempner, Ruth Levy
Papers, 1961–63; 15 inches; MS, typescript, printed, photocopy.

Ruth Levy Kempner (1917–), a native of Galveston, graduated from Ball High School in 1933 and from the University of Texas in

1937. After World War II she became active in political and civic work. Working through the League of Women Voters, Kempner led a movement to restructure the Galveston city charter along the lines of the council-manager form of government. In 1961–63, she served on the first city council elected under the new charter and was the first woman elected to a local governing body in Galveston.

Papers include correspondence, contracts, memoranda, clippings, proposals, reports, policy statements, agendas, and council minutes.

69–0276
E. H. Thornton (Ferry)
Records, 1916–69; 5 inches; MS, typescript, photocopy.

Records and copies of records pertaining to the construction of the ferry *E. H. Thornton* for the Texas Highway Department during 1957–59; the history of the International Shipbuilding Company, 1916–22; and the solicitation of these records by the Rosenberg Library, 1969.

Records are correspondence, contracts, materials lists, and specifications.

70–0017
Pease, Elisha Marshall
Speech, 1880; 25 pages; printed.

Printed copy of a speech delivered by Elisha Marshall Pease, collector of the Port of Galveston. Pease was formerly governor of Texas.

70–0035
Hodson, Rebecca Bell
Letter, August, 1970; 1 page; MS.

Letter concerning James Alexander Minot, captain of the dredge *Texas*, which sank en route to Galveston in 1904. Hodson is the granddaughter of Minot. See also 76–0016.

70–0100—70–0162
Hubbell, Henry
Papers, 1846–65; 5 inches; MS.

Henry Hubbell was a soldier and merchant of Galveston. Our holdings reflect his business and commercial interests, especially the shipping of goods via the Brazos River steamer *William Penn*.

Papers are correspondence, drafts, receipts, statements, notes, and bills of lading.

70–0163—70–0170
First Presbyterian Church
Letters, 1852–53; 8 items; MS.

Letters, statements, and minutes pertaining to a controversy between the board of trustees and B. S. Parsons, church treasurer and Galveston merchant. See also 76–0039.

70–0200—70–0418
Moody, William Lewis
Papers, 1881–95; 10 inches; MS.

Colonel William Lewis Moody, Sr. (1828–1920), was an attorney, soldier, merchant, banker, financier. Our holdings pertain to the activities of Moody as chairman of the Galveston Deep Water Committee, which sought to obtain federal appropriations for harbor improvements at Galveston.

70–0425—70–0474
Galveston Fusileers Battalion
Papers, 1842–43; 50 items; MS.

The Galveston Fusileers Battalion was a volunteer militia company organized in Galveston during 1842.

Holdings include correspondence, a subscription list, a constitution, bylaws, minutes, resolutions, muster rolls, reports, applications and orders, payroll, a narrative of a campaign, court-martial proceedings, and cost estimates for a bridge and levee across Galveston Bay.

70–0475—70–0492
Jack Family
Papers, 1834–64; 18 items; MS.

Correspondence of the family of William H. (1806–44) and Laura Harrison Jack of Brazoria County.

70–0510—70–1138
Hunt, Memucan
Papers, 1831–74; 30 inches; MS.

Deeds, correspondence, invoices, promissory notes, receipts, a partnership agreement, powers of attorney, a notice of protest, telegrams, and memoranda of Memucan Hunt (1807–56), adjutant general of the Somervell expedition, secretary of the navy of the republic of Texas, and a member of the Texas state legislature.

70–1150—70–1178
Cramer, Eliza Anderson
Papers, 1860–66; 29 items; MS.

Correspondence, a receipt, and an abstract pertaining to investments of Eliza Anderson Cramer of Galveston and Poughkeepsie, New York. Efforts to collect on antebellum loans are notable.

70–1179—70–1189
San Luis Company
Records, 1839–43; 11 items; MS, printed.

Promissory note forms (some executed), certificates of property, and an indenture from the land company of the city in Brazoria County.

70–1200—70–1258
Jacques, William Budd
Papers, 1838–62; 59 items; MS.

Correspondence, memoranda, bills, and receipts pertaining to the business of William Budd Jacques, a San Antonio merchant during the period 1839–65.

70–1271—70–1272
Johnson, Albert Sidney
Letters, 1837; 2 items; MS.

Letters from Captain Andrew Neill and Lysander Wells describing army affairs in Colorado Station and San Patricio.

70–1287
Affleck, Thomas Dunbar, Sr.
Papers, 1917–39; 15 inches; MS, typescript, printed.

Thomas Dunbar Affleck, Sr. (1880–1966), a native of Washington County, Texas, was a resident of Galveston from 1913 until his death. He was a cotton broker and real estate agent, as well as a local historian. Papers include letters, notes, clippings, trial balances, cablegrams, shipping receipts, statements, and bills of lading.

71–0162
Ursuline Sisters of Galveston
Report, 1961; 6 pages; typescript.

Report recounting experiences in and damage to Ursuline Convent and Academy during hurricane Carla in September, 1961.

71–0192—71–0195
Fontaine, Sherman A.
Correspondence, 1967; 4 items; MS, typescript.

Letter to Howard Barnstone, architectural historian, from Sherman A. Fontaine describing the Hendley Building in Galveston in 1915–16 and his experiences in the 1915 hurricane. Included are letters from Barnstone to Fontaine and to the Rosenberg Library.

71–0196
Oliver, David T.
Family notes, September 8–14, 1961; 4 pages; typescript.

Notes on experiences of the Oliver family at John Sealy Hospital, at home in Galveston, and at their farm on the west end of the island during the 1961 hurricane. Oliver was an employee of the hospital.

71–0199—71–0206
Stein, Beverley Walden
Poetry, 1940–64; 1 item and 6 volumes; typescript.

Unpublished verse with letter of donation to the library, February 15, 1963.

71–0207
Dreyfus, A. Stanley
Article, 1965; 23 pages; typescript.

Unpublished article on the early history of the Jewish community in Galveston and of the Hebrew Cemetery No. 1.

71–0326—71–0370
Ballinger, William Pitt
Materials, 1846–82; 45 items; MS, printed.

Correspondence concerning the Civil War, editorials, poetry, an address, and a federal license to practice law in 1865–66. Materials were donated by the estate of Thomas G. Rice in 1969. See also 50–0001.

71–0376—71–0383
Smithwick, Edward
Papers, 1860–61; 8 items; MS, pictorial.

Letters containing memoirs and a photograph of Edward Smithwick, Confederate soldier and postwar merchant of Burnet, Morman Mills, and Waco, Texas.

71–0385
Walbridge, Elbridge
Papers, 1836–65; 5 inches; MS, typescript.

A well-known educator of early Galveston, Elbridge Walbridge (ca. 1814–56) became the first school principal in the city in 1839.

He was later president of Galveston University, a private academy organized in 1841. He was also a practicing attorney in Galveston, served on the city council, and was president of the Galveston Lyceum.

Papers are correspondence, diplomas, receipts, deeds, business records, and court documents.

71–0386
Intracoastal Canal
Papers, 1905–75; 5 inches; MS, printed, cartographic.

Clarence S. E. Holland, president of the Victoria Businessmen's Association, organized the Intracoastal Canal Association of Louisiana and Texas to provide a link between Gulf Coast businesses and deepwater ports.

Papers include correspondence, newsletters, pamphlets, booklets, articles, and maps.

71–0387
Adair, A. Garland
Papers, 1935–62; 10 inches; MS, photostat, printed.

Anthony Garland Adair (1889–1966) was born in Queen City, Texas. He graduated from the University of Texas, served in the United States Army during World War I, and was curator of history at the Texas Memorial Museum. He was later executive director of the Texas Heritage Foundation. Adair was coauthor of several books and brochures on Texas history.

Papers consist of correspondence, printed materials, and news clippings.

71–0390
J. Levy & Brother
Cash ledger, 1877–79, and daybook, 1883–89; 5 inches; MS.

Ledger and daybook of the J. Levy & Brother Livery Service & Undertaking Company. Joe and Ben Levy, emigrants from Alsace-Lorraine, established the business in 1868.

The cash ledger has entries for staff salaries, drayage fees, rentals of apartments, and fees for sale of coffins and rental of buggies, carriages, etc. The daybook contains a chronological listing of each burial with an itemized list of services rendered.

72–0001
Texas Navy
Papers, 1836–57; 5 inches; MS, printed.

The papers of the navy of the republic of Texas, including letters, requisitions for supplies, accounts and returns on naval stores, certificates of registry, orders for repairs and outfitting of vessels, court-martial matters, treasury warrants, rosters, and government documents.

72–0102—72–0103
McCutchan, Joseph D.
Diary, 1842–44; 2 volumes; MS.

Diary of Joseph D. McCutchan (1823–53), a member of the Mier expedition to Mexico in 1842–44. Joseph Milton Nance edited the diary and the University of Texas Press published it in 1978.

72–0111—72–0308
Kempner, Isaac H.
Papers, 1940–53; 2½ inches; MS, typescript.

Letters from Isaac Herbert Kempner (1873–1967) to his daughter Cecile, who was a buyer for Lord & Taylor, Inc. Subjects covered in the letters include business affairs, politics, and family concerns.

72–0310
Kempner, Mary Jean
Scrapbook, 1945; 1 volume; printed clippings.

Mary Jean Kempner (1913–69) was a war correspondent for *Vogue* magazine during World War II. The scrapbook contains a series of articles on her experiences in the South Pacific in 1945.

72–0524—72–1992
Sampson, Henry
Papers, 1842–1914; 20 inches; MS, printed.

Henry Sampson (?–ca. 1885) was born in Charleston, South Carolina. He worked for E. J. Hart & Company of New Orleans until 1846, when he bought J. Shackelford, Jr. & Company of Houston. Selling his interest to E. J. Hart & Company in 1853, he became a partner with Benjamin A. Botts in the wholesale mercantile business. At the beginning of the Civil War, Sampson was appointed Confederate produce, loan, and treasury agent for Texas. He came to Galveston in 1868 to become a commission merchant. Sampson was secretary of the Merchants Insurance Company from 1871 to 1876.

Papers consist of correspondence, receipts, deeds, contracts, a will, a stock certificate, clippings, and other business papers.

72–1993
Chataignon, Marius S.
Papers, 1904–76; 2½ inches; MS, printed, pictorial.

A native of France, the Right Reverend Monsignor Marius Stephen Chataignon (1886–1957) entered the priesthood at St. Mary's Cathedral in Galveston in 1911. In 1924, he was appointed pastor of Sacred Heart Catholic Church, Galveston, where he served for thirty-three years. During World Wars I and II, Chataignon was a chaplain, attaining the rank of colonel in the United States Army.

Holdings include incoming correspondence, letters from Chataignon to his sister in Galveston during World War II, clippings, photographs, military records, certificates and awards, and notes and telegrams at the time of his death.

72–1994
First National Bank
Records, 1879–99, 1946–55; 15 inches; MS, typescript.

The First National Bank of Galveston operated from its time of charter in 1865 until it merged with Hutchings-Sealy National Bank in 1958. A distinguished group of early Galvestonians founded the institution. They included Thomas McMahon, George Ball, Allen Lewis, Bivin H. Davis, Levi H. Wood, Prosper B. Shaw, and William Pitt Ballinger.

Our holdings comprise two distinct groups of records. The first, from 1879 to 1899, includes reports to the comptroller of the currency of the United States Treasury. The second group of records covers the period 1946–55. Holdings are ledger and work sheets used in the preparation of reports and tax returns, profit and loss statements, cash short and over statements, dividend and real estate reports, payroll schedules, bond statements, and advertising records.

72–1995
Historic American Buildings Survey
Galveston survey records, 1966–69; 15 inches; MS, printed, typescript, photocopy, cartographic.

Field notes, correspondence, and data assembled by the research team of the second Historic American Buildings Survey of Galveston.

73–0004—73–0007
Gulf City Street Railway & Real Estate Company
Deed of trust and release, 1884, 1885; 4 items; MS.

Deed of trust and release to J. H. Burnett for $5,000 dated July 31, 1884, and January 1, 1885.

73–0055—73–0341
Williams, Henry Howell
Papers, 1839–68; 15 inches; MS, printed.

Henry Howell Williams (1796–1873), brother of Samuel May Williams, settled in Galveston and purchased the mercantile business McKinney & Williams in 1842.

Papers include correspondence, business records, deeds, receipts, contracts, amnesty papers, powers of attorney, insurance policies, and an account book.

73–0342
Stockfleth, Mrs. W. P.
Letters, 1955–56; 3 items; MS, typescript.

Letter from Mrs. W. P. Stockfleth concerning the life of Julius Stockfleth (1857–1935), German-born Galveston painter. The collection also includes two letters of inquiry from the Rosenberg Library.

73–0381
Fort Point Light Station
Journal, 1898–1906; 1 volume; MS.

A log of wind velocities, weather reports, and unusual events in the vicinity of Fort Point.

74–0001
Letitia Rosenberg Women's Home
Records, 1888–1971; 20 inches; MS, printed.

Founded in 1888, this home for aged women merged with the Moody Retirement Center in 1970.

Records include minute books of the board of directors, registers of residents, daybooks, correspondence, resolutions, receipts, and a printed charter and bylaws.

74–0002
O'Connell, Daniel Pius
Papers, 1928–61; 5 inches; MS, typescript, printed, pictorial.

The Right Reverend Monsignor Daniel Pius O'Connell (1890–1966), a native of County Galway, Ireland, came to Texas in 1911 to attend St. Mary's Seminary in La Porte. He entered the priesthood at St. Mary's Cathedral in Galveston in 1914. O'Connell studied canon law at Catholic University of America and became a professor at St. Mary's Seminary in 1915. From 1928 to 1932, he was president of the seminary. He was rector of the cathedral at Galveston for thirty years until his death.

Papers are letters, notes, certificates, speeches, sermons, news clippings, and photographs.

74–0004
Clayton, Nicholas Joseph
Papers, 1874–1915; 5 inches; MS, printed.

Nicholas J. Clayton (1840–1916), the first professional architect in Texas, was associated with the high Victorian school of American architecture. Born in County Cork, Ireland, he came to the United States as a small child. Clayton studied architecture, construction engineering, and sculpture while apprenticed to the firm of Jones & Baldwin of Nashville, Tennessee. In 1871, this firm sent him to Galveston to supervise construction of the Tremont Hotel and the First Presbyterian Church. Upon completion of the Galveston projects, Clayton remained in the city to establish his own architectural firm, N. J. Clayton & Company.

Clayton is known especially for his impressive churches and large, elegant homes and business buildings. His work, however, was quite varied and included some modest frame churches and cottages.

Papers comprise correspondence, a diary, a cash book, a letter-press book, and related papers. The Rosenberg Library also holds architectural drawings by Nicholas Clayton; a separate guide to these is on file in the library.

74–0005
Adoue Foundation
Records, 1909, 1973; 60 items; MS, typescript, photostat.

Minute book, correspondence, deeds, a will, and other documents concerning the Adoue Seamen's Bethel and the Adoue Foundation.

74–0008
J. F. Smith & Brother
Records, 1880–1900; 5 feet; MS.

The Galveston hardware and building supply firm J. F. Smith & Brother was established in 1870. Original partners were John F.

and Edwin A. Smith. After Edwin's death in 1890, J. F. continued to operate the business with the assistance of his four sons Robert, Arthur, Erving, and Wilbur. Following the death of J. F. in 1919, the brothers carried on the business until the sole survivor, Wilbur, sold the firm in 1973.

Records are correspondence, invoices, price quotations, orders, receipts, and applications for employment.

74–0009
Maurer, Joseph M.
Papers, 1911–53; 1 inch; typescript, printed, pictorial, photostat.

Materials relating to the career of Joseph M. Maurer (1876–1953), Galveston photographer, who worked in the studio of Justus Zahn from 1893 to 1896. Following several years of study and travel, Maurer established his own business in 1902. He retired in 1948.

Holdings include programs, pamphlets, bylaws, a code of ethics, and a photograph relating to the Professional Photographers Association of Galveston and the Professional Photographers Association of Texas. The library also holds original prints and negatives by Maurer and his son Joseph I. Maurer.

74–0010
Schadt Family
Papers, 1861–1957; 10 inches; MS, printed, pictorial.

William Fredric Schadt (ca. 1845–1918) was born in Prussia and immigrated to Texas with his parents in the Fisher-Miller expedition of 1846. The parents and three of their children died in the 1847 yellow fever epidemic. During the Civil War, William and his brother Charles were members of John Hood's Texas Brigade.

Letters from the brothers to their sister Caroline in Galveston chronicle their experiences and those of other Galvestonians in the war. Charles died in the Battle of West Point near Williamsburg, Virginia, in May, 1862. William fought in the Battle of Gettysburg, was twice wounded in action, and was taken prisoner.

Returning to Galveston following the war, Schadt worked as a clerk and bookkeeper for lumber and builders' supply houses. In 1885, he married Emma Ida Keller, a Galveston native. By 1888, he operated his own builders' hardware and supply store. Schadt died in Galveston.

Papers consist of letters and notes, deeds, summonses, petitions, newspaper clippings, brigade rosters, voting lists, a tintype, and poems.

74–0011
Galveston Historical Foundation, Ashton Villa Committee
Records, 1965–75; 5 inches; MS, typescript, photocopy, pictorial, graphic.

Records of the Ashton Villa Committee of the Galveston Historical Foundation, which directed the restoration and program development for the 1859 James M. Brown residence.

Records include correspondence, minutes, reports, photographs, and blueprints.

74–0015
Jockusch, John William
Papers, 1847–71; 2½ inches; MS, printed.

John William Jockusch (ca. 1818–98) came to Galveston in 1846. He was the first Galveston resident to obtain naturalization in the new state of Texas and was consul in Galveston for several Germanic governments. His son Julius W. Jockusch (1869–1955) also served as German consul at Galveston.

Papers are certificates of appointment as consul at Galveston from several governments, certifications from the United States government to act as consul, and related documents.

74–0018
Tod, John Grant
Papers, 1830–76; 47½ inches; MS, typescript, printed.

John Grant Tod (1808–77) was a native of Kentucky. After arriving in Texas in 1837, he served the new republic in several capacities. Between 1840 and 1845 he was commander of the naval station at Galveston, secretary of the navy, and commodore of the fleet; he served in the U.S. Navy Quartermaster Department during the Mexican War; he was a founder of the Buffalo Bayou, Brazos & Colorado Railroad; and he also did extensive work on meat and other food processing before and after the Civil War.

Papers are correspondence, receipts, business records, newspaper clippings, and maps.

74–0019
Harris, John W., Jr. and Sr.
Papers, 1848–1918; 9 feet, 2 inches; MS, printed,
letterpress.

Born in Virginia, John Woods Harris, Sr. (1817–87), attended Washington and Lee University and graduated from the University of Virginia Law School in 1837. Following his graduation, Harris moved to Brazoria County, Texas, where he practiced law with John A. Wharton and Elisha M. Pease. In 1839, Harris won a seat in the first congress of Texas. He later served as attorney general of the state under Governors James Pinckney Henderson and George T. Wood. Harris married Annie Pleasant Dallam in 1852. After the Civil War they moved to Galveston, where Harris continued to practice law until his death.

John W. Harris, Jr. (1855–1918), was born in Austin and moved with his parents to Galveston following the Civil War. After graduation from the University of Virginia Law School in 1880, he returned to Galveston and entered the insurance business. During his later life, he invested heavily in Texas real estate.

Papers consist of letters, letterpress volumes of business correspondence, deeds and real estate papers, court briefs, receipts, bills, statements, and estate papers.

75–0001—75–0001a
Hendley, Joseph J.
Letters, 1859, 1864; 4 pages; MS.

Two unrelated business letters (1859 and 1864) to Joseph J. Hendley discuss shipping and the depressed economy in Houston.

Private & confidential
Hermitage
Janry 19th 1844
Genl Saml Houston
President of Texas.
My dear Sir,
I wrote you yesterday which I hope has reached you, on the subject of annexation of Texas to the United States - I have no hesitation to say to you that it is all important for the future prosperity of Texas & the United States that this should be the result.
I have recd this morning from our mutual friend R. J. Walker of the Senate of the United States from Mississippi a letter which I enclose you there are great anxiety with the democratic party in Congress that this annexation should now take place during the present session of Congress - you must recollect how anxious I was, when your independence was acknowledge, to meet your commissioners on this subject, which brought out that old firebrand J. Q. Adams against it - you will see from Mr Walkers letter that it is confidential and you will please, when read and noted to burn it - you will find how Sanguine Mr Walker is of the confirmation of the treaty by the Senate if made. you know I can rely on my friendship & I say to you that such a treaty

This letter from Andrew Jackson to Sam Houston discussed the issue of annexation. "You must recollect how anxious I was . . . to meet your commissioners on this subject, which brought out that old firebrand J. Q. Adams against it."

Galvestonians watched blockading ships from atop the Hendley Building during the Civil War. Built in 1858, the building currently houses the headquarters of the Galveston Historical Foundation.

Beachcombers stroll south of the seawall about 1915. The Hotel Galvez appears in the background.

SKETCHES OF VESSELS IN BLOCKADING SERVICE.
October 1864.

George W. Grover (1819–1901), acting mayor of Galveston during the Civil War, left this illustrated record of vessels in the blockading service in October, 1864.

During the Gilded Age, Galveston's Strand was reputed to be the "Wall Street of the Southwest." Today fine shops and restaurants occupy the restored iron fronts that attract visitors from all parts of the United States.

The Galveston hurricane of 1900 left an estimated six thousand dead. Shown above is the scene on Broadway looking west from Thirteenth Street.

In 1904, Galveston finished the first portion of the seawall, which extended from Sixth Street to Thirty-ninth Street.

Behind the seawall citizens elevated cottages, mansions, and public buildings; deposited fill; and raised the grade of the city.

Members of the Galveston Cotton Exchange surround the trading ring, 1899.

Galveston became the world's largest cotton port in 1906.

Left: Samuel May Williams (1795–1858), secretary for Austin's Colony, director of the Galveston City Company, entrepreneur, banker, and financier of the Texas Revolution. *Right:* Harris Kempner (1837–94), the prototype of the nineteenth-century entrepreneur, immigrated from Poland in 1854. Kempner's interests at his death included real estate, railroading, cotton exporting, and banking.

Sam Maceo, owner of the Balinese Room, with entertainer Carmen Cavallero and Herbert Y. Cartright, colorful mayor of Galveston during the heyday of illegal gambling in the city.

The first city council elected under the new city-manager form of government, 1961. Shown above (seated) are T. D. Armstrong, Ruth Kempner, Robert Albright, Edward Schreiber, Theodore Stubbs, T. A. Waterman, and Ed J. Harris. Standing are city attorney James Phipps and director of public works Owen Holzheuser.

Senator A. R. ("Babe") Schwartz filibusters, about 1978.

75–0002
Galveston–Texas City Pilots
Logbooks, 1891–1902; 3 volumes; MS.

Pilots' ledgers noting the arrivals and departures of ships in Galveston Harbor, April 1, 1891, to January, 1902.

75–0004
Stubbs, James B. and Charles J.
Papers, 1872–1904; 10 feet, 7½ inches; MS, printed.

The brothers James B. (1850–1925) and Charles J. (1867–1948) Stubbs, Galveston attorneys, played important roles in the legal, political, and social life of Galveston during the late nineteenth and early twentieth centuries.

Sons of Theodore Baytop and Catherine Kauffman Stubbs, the brothers were active in the Texas Bar Association, in the Democratic party in Texas, and in social and civic organizations in Galveston. James was admitted to the bar in 1872, upon graduation from Washington and Lee University. He was associated with the firm Ballinger, Jack & Mott until 1889, when he joined his brother Charles in partnership. The Stubbs brothers represented William Sinclair and his interests, including the Beach Hotel and the Galveston City Railroad. They also did legal work for the firm O'Conner, Smoot & Laing, which built the Galveston jetties. When oil was discovered near Beaumont, the Stubbses became actively involved with land and drilling companies.

Separate groups of papers within these holdings include personal correspondence and letters concerning Texas politics, the Texas Bar Association, the Galveston Artillery Company, and other local civic organizations. A large group of papers pertains to the Order of Chosen Friends, a benevolent insurance order organized in the 1870s. Howard H. Morse, a New York attorney who specialized in insurance and corporation law, envisioned this organization to promote his copyrighted Morse Equalization Plan. OCF correspondence covers the years 1885–1902.

In addition to correspondence, the Stubbs collection includes printed materials, letterpress books, notebooks, diaries, case lists, and ledgers.

75–0005
Hurd-Gardner Families
History, 1753–1958; 12 pages; MS, pictorial.

Scrapbook containing photographs and biographical information on the Hurd-Gardner families, who settled in Galveston ca. 1840.

75–0007
Galveston Musical Club
Records, 1897–1974; 20 inches; MS, printed.

The Galveston Musical Club was established by Lucy P. Grunewald, a music teacher, in 1892. The purpose of the club as stated in its constitution was to "provide the best facilities for musical culture of its members and for the uplifting of the standard of music." In 1894, the club was reorganized by Iola Barnes Beers (1853–1925). It was known as the Girls' Musical Club until 1931. The club has sponsored programs by well-known artists as well as recitals by club members.

Records consist of correspondence, programs, minute books, awards, news clippings, financial reports, and portfolios of performers.

75–0008
Centre on the Strand
Records, 1966–72; 20 inches; MS.

Organized by the Junior League of Galveston and located in the First National Bank Building, the Centre on the Strand was a cultural center for the Galveston area. The Galveston County Cultural Arts Council assumed control of the centre in 1972.

Records include project and grant proposals, bylaws, budgets, financial reports, correspondence, board minutes, clippings, reports, associate membership lists, loan agreements, and policy statements.

75–0010
Kempner, Daniel W.
Scrapbooks, 1894–1953; 17½ inches and 1 volume; MS, printed, photocopy.

Daniel Webster Kempner (1877–1956), a native of Galveston, was a leader in the business and social life of the city. He was a trustee of H. Kempner, unincorporated, a director of the United States National Bank, and an officer of Sugarland Industries. He was also active in social, philanthropic, charitable, and religious organizations.

Scrapbooks contain letters, telegrams, invitations, announcements, photographs, and clippings and fragments from newspapers pertaining to the Kempner family and the interests of each member in the family businesses.

75–0013
Savannah (Nuclear ship)
Logbook, 1964; 2 volumes; MS.

Deck logbook of the first transatlantic crossing of the N.S. *Savannah*, April 23–July 28, 1964.

75–0014
McMichael, David B.
Papers, 1964; 2½ inches; MS, typescript, printed, pictorial.

Letters, newspaper clippings, and photographs collected by David B. McMichael, captain of the N.S. *Savannah* during her first transatlantic crossing.

75–0016
McCullough, William Wallace
Papers, 1911–61; 1 inch; MS, pictorial.

Papers donated by William Wallace McCullough pertain to his brief employment on a U.S. Army Corps of Engineers dredge from 1907 to 1911 and to his research concerning the third expedition of Captain John Pope to the Llano Estacado, 1857–59.

75–0017
Stavenhagen, Ernest
Scrapbooks, 1941–58; 4 oversized volumes; MS, printed.

Programs and related materials from choral, oratorial, opera, symphony, musical comedy, ballet, and organ concerts mostly in the Galveston-Houston area, but also in San Antonio, New York, San Francisco, and elsewhere.

75–0019
Galveston Equal Suffrage Association
Records, 1912–20; 2½ inches; MS, printed.

Organized in 1912, this association worked to achieve the vote for women.

Records consist of correspondence, a constitution, programs, proposed legislation, news clippings, press information, pamphlets, and memorabilia.

76–0001
Schott, Justus Julius
Family history, n.d., ca. 1976; 1 volume; photocopy.

Photocopy of an unpublished family history compiled by Christine Schott, daughter of Galveston pharmacist Justus Julius Schott (1846–1928).

76–0003
Zahn Family
Papers, 1827–1939; 5 inches; MS, pictorial, printed.

Justus Zahn (1847–1918), a native of Marburg, Germany, came to the United States in 1869. He returned to Germany the following year to serve in the Franco-Prussian War; after the war, he reentered the United States, establishing a photography studio in Chicago. After some time there he moved to St. Louis and then to Belleville, Illinois, where he married Elise Kreppelt in 1882. Soon thereafter the family came to Galveston. Zahn enjoyed a flourishing business and became well known as a society photographer. Choosing not to remain in Galveston after the hurricane of 1900, the Zahn family moved to St. Louis. In 1909, they moved to Bowling Green, Missouri, where they lived until Justus Zahn's death.

Holdings include correspondence, deeds, marriage certificates, receipts, a will, and photographs. Additional Zahn photographs are in the library's historic photograph collection.

76–0007
Laffite, Jean
Collection, 1813–1957; 10 inches; MS, typescript, photocopy, printed.

An artificial collection consisting of photocopies of original documents, notes of various researchers, and related brochures and booklets on the privateer Jean Laffite (ca. 1781–1826). This collection does not contain original Laffite papers.

76–0011
American Guild of Organists, Galveston Chapter
Records, 1944–76; 5 inches, 1 volume; MS, printed, typescript, photocopy.

The Galveston Chapter of the American Guild of Organists was organized in 1944.

Records are correspondence, contracts, clippings, publicity releases, programs, awards, and certificates.

76–0016
Minot Family
Papers, 1869–1967; 5 inches; MS, printed, cartographic, pictorial.

James Alexander Minot (1835–1931) was an early settler of Hitchcock, Texas, where he retired after a career at sea. The papers also pertain to John Densmore Hodson (1861–1928), who settled in Galveston and married Alice Minot (1871–1945).

The collection consists of correspondence, receipts, a diary, news clippings, telegrams, deeds, estate papers, a ship diary, promissory notes, and a will.

76–0017
Grand Opera House
Programs, 1895–1924; 5 feet, 5 inches; printed.

Programs from the period when the Grand Opera House presented live performances to Galveston audiences.

76–0018
Tremont Opera House
Programs, 1875–1894; 2½ inches; printed.

Printed programs of regular and special performances given at the Tremont Opera House.

76–0019
Political Broadsides and Circulars
Collection, 1898–1927; 2½ inches; printed, typescript.

A collection of local, state, and national campaign materials circulated in Galveston. Topics include wharf strikes, boosterism, the causeway, Negro rights, road improvements, seawall legislation, conservation, municipal bonds, school financing, advertising, and Prohibition.

76–0022
Morris, Suzanne
Papers, 1971–76; 5 inches; MS.

Papers include the manuscript of the novel *Galveston* and the author's correspondence with the Rosenberg Library regarding the book.

76–0023
Harris, Brantly
Papers, 1939–42; 2½ inches; MS, typescript.

Brantly Harris (1893–1942) came to Galveston at the age of two, when his father became pastor of First Baptist Church. In

1921, Harris entered legal practice in the city. He was president of the Galveston Chamber of Commerce, lecturer in medical jurisprudence at the University of Texas Medical Branch, and mayor of Galveston, 1939–42.

Papers consist mostly of correspondence from Mayor Harris to Robert Nesbitt, who represented the Port of Galveston in Washington, D.C. Correspondence concerns wartime needs of the city, military fortifications, recreational facilities for military and civilian personnel, war production, civil defense, and priorities for the construction of public works.

76–0024
Menard, Michel Branamour
Land grant, 1838; 1 page; MS.

Grant from the republic of Texas to Michel B. Menard for a league and a labor of land on the east end of Galveston Island. The document is dated January 25, 1838, and is signed by Sam Houston, president.

76–0026
Napp, Fred
Letter, 1900; 1 page; MS.

Letter dated September 9, 1900, to Maggie Napp from Fred Napp describing the hurricane of 1900.

76–0027
Thompson, Libbie Moody
Papers, 1912–80; 6 feet, 3 inches; MS, printed, pictorial.

Libbie Moody Thompson (1897–), a native of Galveston, married Clark Wallace Thompson in 1918. Since her husband's first term as a United States congressman in 1933, Thompson has been a noted Washington hostess and social figure.

Papers include correspondence, clippings, invitations, greeting cards, programs, pamphlets, guest lists, memoranda, photographs, awards, certificates, scrapbooks, and appointment books.

76–0031
Peter Gengler & Company
Papers, 1911–26; 24 inches; MS, printed.

Correspondence and a scrapbook concerning the diamond jubilee of this Galveston grocery firm in 1926.

76–0032
City of Galveston
Warrant account book, October, 1881–December, 1891; 1 volume; MS.

Record of disbursements for the maintenance of public schools in Galveston, 1881–91.

76–0033
Rosenberg Library
Scrapbooks, 1930–63; 6 volumes; MS, printed.

Scrapbooks pertain to events, operations, and services of the library, 1930–63.

76–0037
Sulzer, William
Scrapbook, 1913–23; 1 volume; MS, printed.

Scrapbook contains letters and printed matter concerning William Sulzer (1863–1941), governor of New York, who took office January 1, 1913, and was impeached October 17, 1913.

76–0038
Shackelford Family
Letters, 1841–69; 5 items; MS.

Letters of the Shackelford family describe social and economic life in Galveston in 1841; travel from Virginia to Ohio in 1848; and personal and legal affairs in 1851 and 1869.

76–0039
First Presbyterian Church
Records, 1868–1976; 35 inches, 9 oversized items; MS, typescript, photocopy, printed.

Established in 1840, the First Presbyterian Church was one of the first Protestant congregations in Galveston.

Records include minutes (1875–79); a list of members and officers, 1930; records of the board of deacons; Sunday school class rosters; Women's Auxiliary records; Ladies' Aid records; financial statements; and scrapbooks. Persons associated with these papers include John McCullough, Evander McNair, Leon Jaworski, E. E. Stavenhagen, Robert Bunting, D. Adriance, and H. F. Young.

Most nineteenth-century records are photocopies of originals in the holdings of the Presbyterian Historical Society, Montreat, North Carolina.

76–0041
Civil War
Scrapbooks, 1861–65; 2 volumes; printed.

These scrapbooks contain newspaper clippings about Civil War battles and events.

76–0042
Galveston Commission Government
Scrapbooks, 1901–13; 5 volumes; MS, printed.

Scrapbooks contain correspondence and news clippings about proceedings and operations of Galveston city government, 1901–13.

76–0044
Spanish-American War
Scrapbook, 1898; 1 volume; printed.

Scrapbook contains political cartoons pertaining to the Spanish-American War, compiled by George Sealy, Sr.

77–0002
Diary of a Union Soldier
Diary, January 1–December 31, 1863; 380 pages; MS.

This anonymous diary was written by a Union soldier taken prisoner in the Battle of Galveston. It includes a list of officers serving on the *Harriet Lane, Morning Light*, and *Velocity* and of officers of the 175th New York Volunteers.

77–0003
Tucker, Philip Crosby
Papers, 1839–1946; 45 inches; MS, typescript, printed.

Philip Crosby Tucker, Jr. (1826–94), a native of Vermont, moved to Galveston and opened a law office there in 1852. During the Civil War, he joined the Confederate army, rising to the rank of major. After the war Tucker returned to Galveston, where he became involved in a variety of civic endeavors. He was a member of the Howard Association (see 14–0030); he was a leader of Freemasonry in Texas; and Tucker and his son, Philip Crosby Tucker III, were both active in the Texas Historical Society of Galveston.

The papers span a variety of subjects and periods of time. They comprise personal and business correspondence and letters that pertain to civic activities. The most extensive subgroup concerns Tucker's lifelong interest in Freemasonry. Included are letters, certificates, and printed matter concerning the Masons in Galveston and Texas. Tucker's first draft of the history of the San Felipe de Austin Chapter of Arch Masons is among the papers.

77–0004
Beissner, Charles L.
Papers, 1847–1918; 75 inches; MS.

Born in Bremen, Germany, Charles L. Beissner, Jr. (1839–1912), immigrated to Galveston as a child. In 1872, he was a cashier with E. W. Hurley & Company, commission merchants. In the early 1880s, Beissner formed a partnership with Robert Irvine of Galveston; and the firm of Irvine & Beissner, brokers and commission merchants, existed until Irvine's death in 1897. At that time Beissner's brother Edward J. joined him in business, and Beissner took on the duties of state and county tax collector. By 1901, the brothers Beissner entered the banking business and became principals in the Rosenberg Bank.

Our holdings reflect several business ventures in which the

Beissners were engaged. Included are correspondence with the office of the state comptroller; assorted papers from the firm of Irvine & Beissner; papers of the estates of Irvine, Henry Rosenberg, George W. Beissner, and Edward L. Ufford; records of the Concordia Society, an exclusive gentlemen's singing society of the late nineteenth and early twentieth centuries; and papers of the Texas Land & Loan Company (1857–1918), one of several land companies through which Galveston businessmen controlled and profited from land development in Texas. The papers show land use patterns throughout the state in a period of development and reflect the position of leadership held by the Galveston business community.

77–0005
Galveston Chamber of Commerce
Records, 1872–1976; 15 inches and 30 items; MS, printed, pictorial.

In addition to a core of early records, papers focus on mid-twentieth-century activities of the chamber. Included are correspondence, guides, rosters of membership, annual reports (1872, 1940–42, 1967, 1972), presidents' reports (1937–41), bulletins, and pamphlets and scrapbooks concerning the Galveston business community, Oleander Festival, Mardi Gras, and publicity contests. Associated people and institutions include the Galveston Commercial Association, the Galveston Cotton Exchange, Meigs O. Frost, Rosella Horowitz Werlin, Jan Isbelle Fortune, the Galveston Community Chest, the Badgett quadruplets, and the University of Texas Medical Branch.

77–0007
Hanna & Fahey Real Estate Agents
Records, 1856–1913; 36 volumes; MS, typescript.

The firm of Hanna & Fahey managed real estate and investments for Galveston individuals and businesses. Material includes cash books, daybooks, letterpress books, and cash and expense ledgers. Persons connected with the records include J. P. Davie, Nicholas J. Clayton, Lucian Minor, Joseph Seinsheimer, Charles L.

Beissner, H. M. Trueheart, John Adriance, Susan Spofford, Morris Lasker, and R. Waverly Smith. Institutions associated with the records include Blum Land Company and the Screwmen's Benevolent Association of Galveston.

77–0011
First Texas Cavalry
Company roll, n.d.; 1 page; MS.

Roll lists officers and privates of this Confederate company.

77–0012
Jackson, Andrew
Letter, 1844; 2 pages; MS.

Signed holograph dated the Hermitage, Nashville, January 19, 1844, to General Samuel Houston, President of Texas, Washington, Texas.

Jackson discusses his feelings regarding the annexation of Texas to the United States.

77–0013
Galveston Customhouse
Records, 1835–46; 2 volumes; MS.

Galveston Customhouse records include a handwritten copy of the ordinance establishing import duties; copies of outgoing correspondence of Gail Borden, collector of customs; ship arrivals and departures; and quarterly records of duty paid.

77–0014
Vidor, King Wallis
Letter, 1919; 1 page; typescript.

Letter dated Los Angeles, California, May 23, 1919, to Ada P. Sweet of Galveston, in which Vidor explains his philosophy of film making as exemplified by his film *The Turn in the Road*.

77–0019
Galveston Gas Company
Minute Book No. 1, 1856–1910; 1 volume; MS.

Records contain an act of incorporation; article of association; minutes of meetings of the board of directors, 1856–1910; a record of stockholders, 1859–80; and scattered correspondence.

77–0021
United Daughters of the Confederacy, Magruder Chapter
Records, 1934–40; 1 volume; MS.

Records include minutes and scattered correspondence of the chapter.

77–0022
Galveston Artillery Company
Minute book, 1881–1900; 1 volume; MS, printed.

Minutes, clippings, invitations, and dance programs from June 9, 1881, to March 6, 1900, of the Galveston Artillery Company, a membership social club.

77–0024
Texas City Disaster
Legal papers, 1947–55; 25 inches; MS, typescript, printed.

A series of explosions at Texas City in April, 1947, killed more than 500 persons.

Our holdings are the papers of a test case brought by the firm of Markwell, Stubbs & Decker that sought to establish the right of families of victims to sue for damages. It was unsuccessful, but congressional action later established this right.

77–0029
League, John Charles
Papers, 1863–1929; 52 feet, 1 inch; MS, printed, cartographic.

John Charles League (1851–1916), a native of Galveston, was the son of Thomas M. League. Educated in Maryland and in Europe, League returned to Galveston at the age of twenty-one to manage the estate of his father. Investing principally in real estate throughout Texas, he became a leading land baron of the period.

Our holdings pertain to League's interests in agriculture, ranching, oil and gas leasing, land investments, and European travels; the papers include letters, statements, leases, contracts, and telegrams. Persons and institutions associated with the papers include Waters S. Davis; Peter Loren; J. T. Harrison; Wolston, Wells & Vidor; C. J. McRae; Mary D. League; the Galveston YWCA; the Galveston Deep Water Committee; and the relief committee for the 1900 hurricanes.

77–0030
127th Coast Artillery
Papers, 1909–44; 2½ inches; MS, printed.

This group of miscellaneous papers of the 127th Coast Artillery contains documents pertaining to activities at Fort Tremont in South Carolina, 1909–14, and Fort Crockett in Galveston, 1915–24. The collection includes general orders, circulars, correspondence, a list of officers, and some printed material.

77–0033
Cahill Cemetery
Records, 1920–77; 20 inches; MS.

Cahill Cemetery, also known as Evergreen Cemetery, was incorporated in 1920. Records include correspondence, incorporation papers, financial reports, and a plot and lot book showing interments from 1923 to 1951.

77–0036
Goals for Galveston
Records, 1969–75; 3 feet, 5 inches; MS, typescript, photocopy, printed.

The Galveston City Council established Goals for Galveston to involve citizens of the community in city planning. The program operated through a goals council, or a board of directors, and committees of citizens who conducted town meetings on various topics. Subjects under discussion were public health, transportation, housing, education, the economy, recreation, public safety, and neighborhood concerns.

Records include correspondence, reports, questionnaires, information sheets, and budgets.

77–0047
Stavenhagen Family
Family tree, 1977; 4 items; photocopy, pictorial.

Genealogy of the Stavenhagen family, compiled by Ernest Stavenhagen.

78–0003
Galveston Historical Society
Records, 1875–1951; 5 inches; MS, printed.

Records of the Galveston Historical Society and its predecessor, the Texas Historical Society of Galveston, include a constitution and bylaws, correspondence, minutes, a list of historical materials held by the society in 1921, scrapbooks, pamphlets, and a history of the society written in 1942. The society donated its local and Texas history collections to the Rosenberg Library in 1931. These materials form the nucleus of the library's archives collection.

78–0009
Rosenberg Bank
Papers, 1848–1925; 10 inches; MS.

The Rosenberg Bank was the successor firm to the Galveston Bank & Trust Company, which Henry Rosenberg controlled from 1876 until his death in 1893. In 1882, Rosenberg changed the name of the bank to Henry Rosenberg, Banker; and in 1894 the name was changed to the Rosenberg Bank. The institution continued in operation until it merged with South Texas State Bank in 1913.

The holdings pertain to bank customers and include tax receipts, licenses, estate papers, checks, and drafts.

78–0011
Galveston Quartette Society
Records, 1891–1917; 2 inches and 39 items; MS, typescript, printed, pictorial.

Records of this theatrical society include rules and bylaws, programs, a broadside, and photographs of people and productions.

78–0012
H. M. Trueheart & Company
Letterpress volumes, 1866–1909; 32 feet, 6 inches; letterpress.

Founded by Henry Martyn Trueheart (1832–1914), this firm traces its beginnings to his appointment as tax assessor and collector of Galveston County in 1857. Trueheart, a native of Virginia, served in the Confederate army. During Reconstruction, he established a real estate business, which he later expanded to include land promotion, leasing, tax collection, foreclosure, and financing. Eventually the company managed estates, made loans, and wrote insurance; because of widespread national and international advertising and correspondence, it influenced patterns of migration, immigration, and settlement throughout Texas during the late nineteenth century. In 1905, John Adriance bought controlling interest in the firm and changed the name to John Adriance & Sons.

The holdings reflect the business and civic endeavors of Trueheart. He was an officer or board member of the Galveston Wharf Company, Galveston school board, Texas Guarantee & Trust Company, Southern Cotton Press Company, the First Presbyterian Church, and the Galveston Land & Improvement Company. Holdings are letterpress books containing copies of outgoing letters, statements, and tax notices.

78–0013
H. M. Trueheart & Company
Ledgers, 1859–1908; 89 items; MS.

Holdings include lease books, collection books, real estate agents' books, daybooks, cash books, tax journals, tax assessment rolls, estate ledgers, receipt books, trial balances, and acknowledgments registers.

78–0014
H. M. Trueheart & Company
Papers, 1865–1904; 130 feet, 10 inches; MS.

Holdings include letters, notes, deeds, receipts, powers of attorney, wills, telegrams, and invoices.

78–0017
John Adriance & Sons
Papers, 1905–36; 16 feet, 3 inches; MS, printed.

John Adriance & Sons, the successor firm to H. M. Trueheart & Company, Realtors, existed in Galveston from 1905 until 1969. The records of both firms reflect land use in Texas in the late nineteenth and early twentieth centuries. Especially notable in the Adriance collection are records pertaining to oil and gas exploration in southeast Texas during the early 1900s and to dust bowl conditions in west Texas in the 1930s.

Records include correspondence, receipts, contracts, statements, estate papers, and leases.

78–0018
Galveston County Scholastic Census
Records, 1900–12; 20 feet, 5 inches; MS.

This annual survey of school-aged children is arranged chronologically by year; thereunder by town, district, or race; and thereunder alphabetically. Census information includes the name of each child and his/her age, sex, nationality, and date of birth; the name of the parent or guardian registering the child and his/her nationality; the date of registration; and the name of the school or school district.

78–0019
Patten, Frank C.
Papers, 1878–1934; 4 feet, 2 inches; MS, printed, pictorial.

Frank C. Patten (1855–1934) was the first librarian of the Rosenberg Library. He accepted the appointment a year before the library opened in 1904, and he served until his death. A native of Rochester, New York, Patten grew up in Wisconsin, where he attended Oshkosh State Normal School and Ripon College. He was the assistant librarian at Ripon when he applied to Melvil Dewey to join the first class of the Columbia College School of Library Economy. He graduated in Dewey's first class in 1887 and spent an additional two years in training there. After working for three years as a cataloger at the New York State Library, Patten moved to Helena, Montana, where he was the director of the public library for seven years. He left Helena to attend Harvard graduate school. Just prior to Patten's appointment to the directorship of the Rosenberg Library, he was the assistant librarian at the Lenox Branch of the New York Public Library.

Papers include correspondence, daybooks, promissory notes, college papers, diplomas, awards, notebooks, news clippings, bank account books, real estate records, receipts, statements, a will, photographs, and insurance papers.

78–0021
Lasker Home for Children
Records, 1904–60; 2 feet, 6 inches; MS.

The Lasker Home for Children is the successor institution to the Society for Friendless Children, which was established in 1894. After a sizable donation from Galvestonian Morris Lasker in 1912, the organization adopted the name of its benefactor.

Records include minutes, financial records, and correspondence.

78–0022
Moore, Hugh B.
Papers, 1897–1950; 7½ inches; MS, printed.

Hugh B. Moore (1874–1944) came to Dallas at the age of fifteen to work in various jobs in railway and steamship firms. In 1905, he became general manager of the Texas City Terminal Railway Company; he became president of the firm in 1919. During World

War I, Moore received the commission of captain in the United States Army. He served for two years as general superintendent and director of Army Transport Service in France. Moore spent a lifelong career in railway, port terminal, and steamship service and was a traveling adviser to military port-of-embarkation directors during World War II. He was a strong advocate of a centralized, synchronized national transportation network.

Papers include official orders and correspondence of the Army Transport Service, 1917–18; correspondence with the War Department, 1942–44; and investment papers, telegrams, and biographical information on Moore.

78–0023
Harris, Ed J.
Papers, 1963–76; 14 feet, 2 inches; MS, typescript, printed, pictorial.

Ed J. Harris (1920–), born in Trinity, Texas, moved with his family to Galveston, where he attended public schools. In 1941, he graduated from Southwestern University in Georgetown, Texas. During World War II, Harris joined the navy and served as a pilot until 1946. Retaining a reserve commission, he attained the rank of commander in the U.S. Navy. In 1961, Harris ran successfully for the first Galveston City Council under the newly adopted council-manager plan. After serving one year, he retired from the council to become Galveston's representative in the Texas legislature. Serving for fifteen years in the state House of Representatives, Harris was chairman of the Elections Committee (1973) and was on fifteen other committees at various times and for varying periods. In 1971, he was a leader of the "Dirty Thirty," a group of liberal representatives who ousted conservative Speaker of the House Gus Mutscher. Harris was also a member of the 1974 Texas constitutional convention. Upon leaving the legislature, he was elected judge of the Tenth Judicial District Court at Galveston.

The papers comprise five groups: legislative papers, 1975–76; Texas constitutional convention papers, 1974–75; legislative papers, 1973–74; legislative papers, 1963–73; and scrapbooks.

78–0024
Schwartz, A. R.
Papers, 1955–80; 65 feet; MS, printed, pictorial.

Aaron Robert Schwartz (1926–) was born in Galveston. After completing law school in 1951, he served as assistant attorney of Galveston County. Schwartz was a member of the Texas House of Representatives, 1954–60, and of the Texas Senate, 1960–80. During his tenure in the legislature, he served on nearly every major committee. He was the author of legislation on a wide range of subjects including mental health, coastal and environmental protection, revision of narcotics laws, public education, equal rights, and insurance. He was a member of the Texas constitutional convention of 1974 and of the liberal coalitions, the "Dirty Thirty" and the "Killer Bees."

Papers are legislative materials, including correspondence to and from constituents, bills, resolutions, amendments, notes, research, and supporting material. Original order is retained; organization is chronological by subject, with all materials filed together under each subject.

78–0025
Rosenberg Bank
Volume series, 1850–1925; 350 items; MS.

Holdings are records of businesses, organizations, and people with whom Henry Rosenberg was associated: H. Rosenberg, Banker; the Rosenberg Bank; Galveston Bank & Trust Company; South Texas State Bank; Strussy & Blum; Texas Land & Loan Company; Charles L. Beissner; Texas Guarantee & Trust Company; Thompson & Ohmstede; M. Lewis; Galveston Cycle Club; J. W. Riddell, Banker; Sea Shore Lodge No. 62; National City Bank of New York; and Chatham & Phoenix.

Records include trial balance ledgers; merchandise, stock, invoice, sales, and shipment books; cash books; collection and deposit registers; tellers' and clearing books; bills payable and receivable journals; real estate and insurance books; and records of Rosenberg's dry goods business.

78–0026
Little Theatre of Galveston
Records, 1921–53; 25 inches and 6 volumes; MS, printed,
pictorial.

The records of the Little Theatre include correspondence,
statements, minutes, contracts, scrapbooks, programs, clippings,
and photographs. The majority of the holdings date from the early
period of the organization, 1931–34. The theater reorganized following liquidation in the 1930s, and it enjoyed another flourishing
period in the late 1940s and early 1950s.

78–0027
Rosenberg Bank
Letterpress books, 1856–1917; 18 feet, 9 inches; letterpress,
typescript.

Outgoing correspondence of Henry Rosenberg, dry goods
merchant and banker, and his business. Letters include communi-
cations with banks in New York and St. Louis and with firms and
persons throughout Texas.

78–0028
League of Women Voters
Records, 1907–67; 1 foot, 10½ inches; MS, typescript,
printed.

Active in Galveston since 1919, the League of Women Voters
has been a leading force in civic and political affairs. Records include correspondence, flyers, brochures, policy statements, study
reports, handbooks, speeches, press releases, and scrapbooks. Some
of the subjects and institutions included are the Galveston Independent School District, Galveston City Charter Committee, commission and council-manager forms of government, and Texas League
of Women Voters.

79–0000
First Baptist Church
Records, 1840–1938; 5 inches; MS.

Established in 1840, this is the oldest Baptist congregation in
Galveston. The records include a church treasurer's account book

(1924), building fund records (1882), Sunday school class rosters, minute books, and reports. The library also has a microfilm copy of church minutes, 1840–83.

79–0001
Trinity Episcopal Church
Records, 1918–44; 15 inches; MS, printed.

Statements and financial reports, parochial reports, warden and vestry reports, trust fund audits, Episcopal cemetery agreements, pledges, records of the Women's Auxiliary, and budgets for Trinity Episcopal Church in Galveston.

79–0004
J. P. Davie & Company
Records, 1869–1913; 13 volumes; MS.

The J. P. Davie & Company hardware firm, which later engaged in the commission merchant business, opened in Galveston in 1840 under the name Wilson & Davie. Our holdings include cash books, daybooks, letterpress books, and account books from the hardware business.

79–0005
Rosenberg Library
Papers, 1871–1979; 48 feet, 7 inches; MS, typescript, printed, pictorial.

The Rosenberg Library, the oldest public library in Texas in continuous operation, is the successor institution to the Galveston Mercantile Library established in 1871. Henry Rosenberg, banker and philanthropist, bequeathed the bulk of his estate to the city of Galveston for the public library, which bears his name.

Holdings include staff correspondence, borrowers' registers, broadsides, scrapbooks, brochures, records of exhibits and meetings held in the library, and records of construction and renovation of the building.

79–0006
Stubbs, Theodore B.
Mayoral papers, 1962–64; 20 inches; MS, typescript, printed.

Theodore B. Stubbs (1907–) was a leader of the movement to adopt the council-manager plan for the city of Galveston. He was a member of the City Charter Commission, which drafted the plan in 1959–60. In 1961, he ran successfully for the first city council elected under the new charter. He was mayor of Galveston in 1962–63. Stubbs, a prominent attorney in Galveston, is associated with the firm of Markwell & Stubbs. He has served as president of the Galveston County Bar Association, was a member of the Galveston County Democratic Executive Committee, and has been president of the University of Texas Ex-Students Association. In addition, he has been active in Catholic activities in the city and has served as a member of the board of St. Mary's Orphanage.

Papers include official correspondence, policy statements, budgets, notes, and correspondence pertaining to local issues.

79–0007
Galveston Garden Club
Records, 1931–67; 7½ inches; MS, typescript, printed, pictorial.

Correspondence, scrapbooks, membership and officers lists, bylaws, financial reports, programs, and publicity of the club, which was established in 1938.

79–0008
Galveston, City of
Papers, 1887–1953; 5 inches; MS.

This collection contains miscellaneous records from various departments of the city of Galveston. A major portion of the papers concerns the plan for a new city water supply in the early 1890s.

Papers are correspondence, reports, petitions, receipts, a payroll list, memoranda, and telegrams.

79–0009
Fox, Warren F.
Papers, 1920–72; 5 inches; MS, typescript, pictorial, cartographic.

Warren F. Fox, M.D. (1890–1952), was born in Flushing, New York. In 1918, he moved to Galveston, where he was the director of the United States Public Health Service Quarantine Station. He left Galveston in 1921 to serve as health officer for various cities and counties in southern California.

Our holdings include, almost exclusively, a three-hundred-page illustrated manuscript for an unpublished book, "Our Enemy, the Rat." Fox wrote the manuscript after he left Galveston, but he conducted his research and experiments in this city.

79–0010
Naylor Family
Papers, 1862–1933; 5 inches; MS, printed.

Isaac Naylor (1824–85), a descendant of early Quaker settlers in Philadelphia, was born in Ohio. In 1851, he moved to Galveston, where he established a school. In 1858, he married Henrietta Wood, daughter of hardware merchant E. S. Wood of Galveston. Naylor later settled in Dallas, where he practiced law.

Papers include manuscript and published genealogies of the Naylor and related families, and correspondence pertaining to family history.

79–0011
Toebelman Family
Papers, 1851–1922; 5 inches; MS, typescript.

Henry Toebelman (1837–1923), a native of Bremen, Germany, immigrated to New Orleans in 1854. After working briefly as a clerk on a Morgan Line steamship, he settled in Galveston. Enlisting in the Confederate army at the outbreak of the Civil War, Toebelman was a leader of Cook's Heavy Artillery Band. In 1866, he married Elizabeth Jersig, who was born in Austria and came to Galveston in 1845, at the age of ten. Following the war, he worked as a bookkeeper for F. Halff & Company, later Halff, Weis & Company. In the early 1870s, Toebelman established a wholesale shoe leather and bindings company, which carried the family name. In 1885, he started the Galveston Steam Shoe Factory, which he operated until the 1900 hurricane.

Papers are letters from friends and family members, the earliest of which are in German; business correspondence; receipts from Toebelman & Company; and miscellaneous papers including deeds, estate papers, a land grant, a will, and bank statements.

79–0012
Port of Galveston
Papers, 1890–1958; 5 inches; MS, printed.

Manuscript and printed documents of the Galveston Wharf Company include authorizations to deliver company bonds, charter and bylaws, annual reports, a 1901 folder on Galveston Harbor for the Trans-Mississippi Commercial Congress, Interstate Commerce Commission actions regarding the Port of Galveston, news clippings, correspondence, agreements, letters to stockholders, and examples of greeting cards used by the port. See also 81–0014.

79–0013
Texas Guarantee & Trust Company
Papers, 1870–1917; 5 inches; MS, printed.

Papers of the Texas Guarantee & Trust Company include bylaws, a list of stockholders, balances, bills receivable, estate papers, deeds, debt settlements, powers of attorney, liquidation papers, partnership papers, receipts, checks, and drafts.

79–0014
Thompson, Thomas C.
Papers, 1836–1906; 5 inches; MS.

Thomas C. Thompson, M.D., (1839–98), was a member of the first board of managers of John Sealy Hospital, and he later served as president of that board.

Holdings include the estate papers of Isham Thompson and receipts, notes, releases, sale notices, deeds, and drafts pertaining to drug and real estate interests of Dreiss, Thompson & Company; San Antonio Drug Company; Orynski, Thompson & Company; Thompson & Ohmstede; and Thompson Drug Company.

79–0015
Johnson, Frank C.
Papers, 1921–62; 5 inches; MS, printed, pictorial.

Frank C. Johnson (1891–1970) was an educator who worked in the Galveston Independent School District for over fifty years. During his career he was a teacher at Ball High School, and he was principal of San Jacinto Elementary, Stephen F. Austin Junior High, and Ball High schools. His civic activities included the American Red Cross and Freemasonry.

Papers include educational certificates, unpublished articles, Masonic correspondence, and letters regarding his professional career.

79–0016
Bond Family
Papers, 1831–1965; 15 inches; MS, pictorial.

Correspondence, receipts, wills, tax returns, deeds, stock certificates, contracts, and photographs of the Bond, Hassmann, Fassbender, Ollre, Allien, and Lockhart families.

79–0017
Dyer, Joseph Osterman
Papers, 1871–1926; 5 inches; MS, graphic.

Papers include Dyer's published and unpublished articles on Galveston and Texas history. His favorite topics were pirates, plagues, native tribes, early Texas newspapers, the Texas Republic, and primitive medicine. See also 26–0402.

79–0018
University of Texas Medical Branch
Materials, 1879–1948; 2½ inches; printed.

The Texas Medical College and Hospital was established in 1873 as a reorganization of the original Galveston Medical College, founded in 1864. The University of Texas Medical Branch, established in 1890, succeeded the Texas Medical College and Hospital.

Our research collection consists of a commencement program, an announcement of the 1888 reopening of the Texas Medical College and Hospital, and catalogs, rosters of students, and commencement announcements and programs from the Medical Branch.

79–0019
Cooper, Bayliss P.
Papers, 1843–1910; 10 inches; MS.

Bayliss P. Cooper (ca. 1834–1907) was a native of Mobile, Alabama. He settled in Galveston and was a blockade runner during the Civil War. After the war he operated several transportation companies and was a captain of vessels operating on Galveston Bay and the Trinity River. In later life Cooper lived in Galveston, where he invested in real estate.

Holdings include correspondence, bank books, tax receipts, wills, estate papers, court records, and real estate abstracts.

79–0020
Marburger, Marie
Papers, 1916–69; 2½ inches; MS, typescript, printed.

A native of Cistern, Texas, Marie Marburger (1903–79) joined the Rosenberg Library staff in 1921 and remained there until she went to the University of Texas in the late 1930s. After graduating from the University in 1942, she returned to the Rosenberg Library. From then until her retirement, Marburger held nearly every position in the public services division of the library. In 1966, she was appointed to the new position of curator; and in 1968, she retired.

Correspondents include Frank C. Patten, Phyllis Gugett, Margaret Gahagan, Mrs. J. E. Jackson, Mrs. W. Warmoth, J. S. Ibbotson, W. A. James, Mary Gardner, Elizabeth Leake, Bertha Fritz, Lucy Stiefel, Mildred M. Oser, Ray Fry, Anne Brindly, Mrs. Louise E. Reifel, Francis Nicol, Peter J. LaValle, Mrs. Paul Heinrich, Velma Bradshaw, Donald T. Peak, Bob Cunningham, William R. Holman,

Charles O'Halloran, Clark W. Thompson, Mrs. Lloyd F. Sanborn, Jr., and O. T. Baker.

79–0021
Penland, Samuel M.
Autograph album, 1808–1921; 1 volume; MS.

The Penland collection was part of the estate of Samuel M. Penland (1845–1922), a nephew of Sam Houston. Included are autographs and signed letters of eighty persons of local, national, and international importance. Notable correspondents include Harriet Beecher Stowe, Sam Houston, Andrew Jackson, John Quincy Adams, Garibaldi, and Horace Greeley.

79–0022
Galveston City Party
Records, 1919–33; 10 inches; MS, printed.

Organized in 1919, the Galveston City party was one of several local political factions active in the 1920s and 1930s. Leading members were representatives of the Kempner and Sealy families, who were influential in the Galveston Wharf Company.

Papers include election notices, platform statements, press releases, correspondence, and news clippings.

79–0024
Mann & Baker
Records, 1870–83; 5 inches; MS, printed.

Records are from the office of Mann & Baker, a law firm active in Galveston from 1867. Principals of the partnership were George E. Mann and Presley C. Baker.

Records include memoranda books of both partners, docket books, manuscript notes, and a printed brief with manuscript notes.

79–0026
Wimhurst Family
Papers, 1880–1955; 20 inches; MS.

Frederick Wimhurst (1858–1932) was a native of England. In 1894 he married Anna Moser (1868–1955), the daughter of a pioneer Galveston family. In 1882, Wimhurst established a paint firm that remained in his family for the next eighty years. In the early twentieth century, the business expanded to include contracting and real estate.

Papers include correspondence, receipts, marriage and death notices, wills, income tax returns, insurance policies, bank statements, stock certificates, deeds, contracts, leases, and business record books.

79–0027
Crocket, George F.
Papers, 1843–1900; 20 inches and 8 volumes; MS.

Papers are cash journals, correspondence, estate papers, notes, court cases, inventories, and daybooks from the mercantile business of George F. Crocket in San Augustine, Texas.

79–0028
Galveston-Niigata Committee
Records, 1964–76; 5 inches; MS, printed.

Records of the Galveston-Niigata Committee include minutes, correspondence, articles, news clippings, and a scrapbook pertaining to the sister-city project.

79–0029
Campbell-Fuller Family
Papers, 1857–1964; 20 inches and 1 volume; MS, printed.

Andrew Monroe Campbell (1812–86) was a native of North Carolina. In 1850, he settled in Colorado County, Texas, where he became a landowner and a county judge. Following the Civil War he moved to Galveston and established Campbell & Clough, cotton factors and commission merchants. He married a Galveston teacher, Virginia Williams, and they had two daughters, Bessie and Alice. Alice (1868–1964) married Aubrey Fuller, an assistant district attorney of Galveston County.

The family papers include correspondence, receipts, bank

statements, certificates, licenses, genealogical notes, newspaper clippings, a will, poetry, diaries, scrapbooks, autograph books, recipe books, and address books.

79–0030
Ragsdale, Silas B.
Papers, 1896–1974; 5 inches; MS.

Silas Ragsdale (ca. 1897–1976) was the managing editor of the *Galveston Daily News*, 1923–44. He left the *News* to become an editor for the Gulf Publishing Company in Houston.

The collection contains correspondence, receipts, notes, and news articles and stories by Ragsdale.

79–0031
Osterman Widows and Orphans Home Fund
Records, 1936–51; 5 inches; MS.

Holdings consist of correspondence and financial records.

79–0033
Cohen, Henry
Papers, 1890–1952; 5 inches; MS, typescript, photocopy, printed.

Henry Cohen (1863–1952) was a native of London, England. He attended Jews' Hospital and Jews' College, and he was ordained a rabbi in 1884. After leading congregations in Kingston, Jamaica, and Woodville, Mississippi, he arrived in Galveston in 1888 to head Temple B'Nai Israel. He remained there until his death. Throughout Cohen's career he was a leader in humanitarian causes. He organized relief for the poor; he was the local organizer of the Galveston Immigration movement, which relocated some ten thousand Eastern European Jews to new homes in Texas and the Southwest; and he was an early advocate of prison reform.

Papers include correspondence, telegrams, a scrapbook, programs, clippings, lecture notes, articles, reprints, and poetry. Extensive collections of Cohen papers are at the University of Texas in Austin and the American Jewish Archives in Cincinnati.

79–0034
Lovenberg Junior High School
Records, 1934–76; 15 inches; MS, printed.

Holdings consist of correspondence, financial records, a student handbook, parent-teacher association minutes, scrapbooks, and student newspapers.

79–0035
Franklin, Joseph
Records, 1838–1908; 2 volumes; MS.

Records of death, powers of attorney, and general information concerning certain residents of Galveston.

79–0036
Galveston City Sexton
Records, 1859–73, 1878–84; 2 volumes; MS.

Records of interments of the Galveston city sexton comprise name, cause and date of death, date and place of burial, and age, sex, race, residence, and nativity of each person buried.

Volume 1 was transcribed and published by Peggy H. Gregory of Houston in 1976.

79–0037
Committee for Pier 19
Records, 1973–78; 15 inches; MS, typescript, printed, pictorial, cartographic.

These records concern the decision of the board of trustees of the Galveston wharves to relocate the "mosquito fleet" (shrimp and party boats) from Pier 19 to Pelican Island, in order to improve facilities of Pier 19 to accommodate ocean-going vessels. Records also cover the efforts of the Pier 19 tenants to confront the board decision by forming a committee of interested persons.

These papers were donated by Ralph Woods, a leading member of the Committee for Pier 19. Records include correspondence, notes, minutes, copies of city ordinances, clippings, and drawings pertaining to the campaign to save Pier 19 for the mosquito fleet.

80–0001
First Hutchings-Sealy National Bank
Ledgers, 1875–1966; 54 volumes; MS.

Records include minutes, stock certificates, securities ledgers, news clippings, bond records, real estate certificates, cash books and general ledgers of the First Hutchings-Sealy National Bank and these predecessor institutions: Galveston Bank & Trust Company, 1875–77; Ball, Hutchings & Company, 1886–1901; South Texas National Bank, 1913–27; Hutchings, Sealy & Company, 1904–58; First National Bank of Galveston, 1915–66; and Hutchings Joint Stock Association, 1917.

80–0002
Kempner Family
Papers, 1930–69; 55 feet; MS, printed, typescript.

80–0003
H. Kempner, Unincorporated
Records, 1870–1968; 245 feet; MS, printed, typescript, cartographic, pictorial.

Harris Kempner (1837–94) emigrated from Poland in 1854 and settled in Cold Spring, Texas. In 1857, he opened a small business, which was interrupted by service in the Confederate army during the Civil War. Having returned to Cold Spring after the war, Kempner moved to Galveston in 1870. There he joined Max Marx in the wholesale grocery business. During the years that followed, Marx and Kempner expanded the business to include cotton factoring. They dissolved the partnership in 1883, but Kempner continued the business interests formed earlier.

In 1885, Kempner entered banking when the board of directors of the Island City Savings Bank asked him to assume the presidency of the financially troubled institution. During the years before his death, Kempner expanded his investments to include real estate and railroading, as well as cotton factoring and banking.

When Harris Kempner died, his son Isaac Herbert Kempner (1873–1967) assumed leadership of the family business known thereafter as H. Kempner, unincorporated. In this period the business was active in railroading, insurance, ranching, oil, land development, sugar, and cotton.

In 1902, H. Kempner, unincorporated, purchased the controlling interest in the Island City Savings Bank and changed the name to the Texas Bank & Trust Company. When the bank charter expired in 1923, the Kempner family secured a charter from the federal government for a national bank. They changed the name to the United States National Bank, the last institution in the United States to use this name.

In 1907, I. H. Kempner and W. T. Eldridge purchased the Cunningham Sugar Company of Ft. Bend County and renamed it Imperial Sugar Company. A trust estate, Sugarland Industries, was formed in 1919 and reorganized in 1948.

Throughout the second generation of the business, I. H. Kempner and his three brothers, Daniel W. Kempner (1877–1956), R. Lee Kempner (1883–1966), and Stanley E. Kempner (1885–1954), managed the business by unanimous consent. Each had an area of expertise: I. H. managed the cotton business and the administration of the whole; Daniel W. administered building and the Merchants & Planters Compress & Warehouse Company; Lee was president of the United States National Bank; and Stanley was president of the Texas Prudential Insurance Company.

At this writing four family members are involved in the administration of H. Kempner: Harris L. Kempner, Sr. (1903–), son of I. H.; Harris L. Kempner, Jr. (1940–); I. H. Kempner III, nephew of Harris; and Daniel Oppenheimer, nephew of I. H.

Nineteenth-century records are those of Marx & Kempner and M. Marx & Company. These concern ranching and land promotion. The records of Imperial Sugar Company and, later, Sugarland Industries begin in 1907. Cotton records are virtually complete beginning in the 1920s, and these compose the single greatest holding. For the business scholar, they detail all the procedural intricacies behind worldwide cotton transactions, including crop gathering, classing, compress work, buying and selling, rail and maritime shipping, and international monetary exchange methods.

The personal papers of the Kempner family include correspondence, which formerly was interfiled with the business records.

The personal collection is arranged chronologically, and the business records are chronological by subject. Both collections are open, except for the most recent twenty-five years.

80–0004
Schlutter & Blanton, Lumber
Cashbook, 1865–69; 1 volume; MS.

Financial records of the Schlutter & Blanton lumber firm, 1865–69.

80–0005
Beta Study Club
Records, 1929–79; 5 inches; MS.

The Beta Study Club of Galveston grew out of the Beta Delphia Chapter of the Delphian Society, which was organized locally in 1929. Adult education, personal improvement, and social exchange are the primary goals of the women's organization.

Records include minutes and yearbooks.

80–0006
Galveston Volunteer Service Bureau
Records, 1948–61; 10 inches; MS.

Financial records of the bureau, which coordinated volunteer social services in the city. Records include bank statements, monthly reports of finances, and income tax withholding forms.

80–0007
Morgan Family
Papers, ca. 1880–ca. 1960; MS, printed, pictorial.

Materials of George Dickinson Morgan (1862–1942), his wife Jean Scrimgeour Morgan (1868–1938), and other family members. Holdings are closed pending completion of processing.

94

80–0008
Morgan, William Manning
Papers, ca. 1930–60; MS.

Papers of William Manning Morgan (1891–1957) and research materials pertaining to his 1954 publication, *Trinity Protestant Episcopal Church, Galveston, Texas, 1841–1953: A Memorial History*. Holdings are closed pending completion of processing.

80–0009
Talleyrand, Charles Maurice de
Letter, 1829; 1 item, MS.

Signed holograph dated December 16, 1829, from Charles Maurice de Talleyrand (1754–1838) to his employee. The letter pertains to personal business of the prince.

80–0010
Bruer, Thomas D.
Land patent, 1830; 1 item; MS.

Patent is dated December 8, 1830, in Washington, D.C. The document, which is signed by Andrew Jackson and Elijah Haywood, commissioner of the General Land Office of the United States, grants a tract of land at Palestine, Illinois, to Thomas D. Bruer of Mason County, Kentucky.

81–0001
Colombo, LeRoy
Scrapbooks, 1928–80; 2 volumes; MS, typescript, printed, pictorial.

LeRoy Peter Colombo (1905–74) was a deaf-mute lifeguard credited with saving more than 1,000 lives on Galveston beaches during a forty-year career.

Materials are newspaper clippings, letters to Colombo and his family, programs, photographs, and a memorial book.

81–0003
Kelley, William D.
Papers, 1853–86; 39 items; MS, typescript.

William D. Kelley (1825–88) was a Galveston physician and surgeon. In 1879 and 1883, he accompanied John Sealy and Leon

Blum on travels through the western United States and Europe. Letters to Kelley's wife and family describe the excursions and the trip that Kelley took by himself in 1886. See also 27–0019— 27–0022.

81–0007
Morgan, Leon A.
Papers, 1937–78; 20 inches; MS, typescript, photocopy, printed.

Leon A. Morgan (1909–), retired administrator for Galveston Independent School District, was associated with education in Galveston for over forty years as a classroom teacher, principal, and director of instruction and curriculum. Throughout his career he was especially active in community service and in statewide educational organizations.

Holdings include correspondence, reports, notes, surveys, speeches, and research materials.

81–0014
Galveston Wharf Company
Records, 1854–1943; 40 items; MS.

Incorporated in 1854 as the Galveston Wharf & Cotton Press Company, the company changed its name in 1860 to Galveston Wharf Company. Since 1940 the wharves have been a wholly owned agency of the city of Galveston.

Holdings include books of minutes of directors' meetings, journals, time and payroll books, reports to stockholders, cashbooks, stock ledgers, and a scrapbook. See also 79–0012.

82–0001
Galveston Cotton Exchange
Records, 1884–1949; 8 volumes and 15 inches; MS, typescript.

Founded in 1872, the Galveston Cotton Exchange was the first west of the Mississippi River. Records are minutes of meetings of the board of directors.

Index

Abercrombie, L. A., 72–0524—72–1992
Abilene, Texas, 70–0200—70–0418; 74–0019
Acheson, Sam H., 62–0003—62–0200
Ackerman & McMillam, 22–0153—22–0246
Adair, A. Garland, papers, 71–0387
Adams, Charles C., 78–0014
Adams, J. W., 72–0001
Adams, John Quincy, 79–0021
Adkins, Leslie, 29–0028—29–0243
Adler, Sophie, 77–0003
Adoue, Bertrand, 74–0005
Adoue & Lobit, 78–0014; 79–0012
Adoue Foundation, papers, 74–0005
Adoue Seamen's Bethel, 74–0005
Adriance, Carroll, 78–0017
Adriance, Corneil Davis, 78–0017
Adriance, John, Jr., 22–0023
Adriance, John, & Sons, 22–0153—22–0246; 78–0014; papers, 78–0017
Affleck, Thomas, 23–0002—23–4503; papers, 33–0004—33–0012e
Affleck, Thomas Dunbar, papers, 70–1287
Affleck's Southern Nurseries, 23–0002—23–4503
Affleck's Southern Rural Almanac, 23–0002—23–4503
Afro-Americans. *See also* Slavery
—civil rights, 41–0002—41–0005; 76–0019
—education, 04–0049—04–0050; 79–0005; 81–0007
—labor contracts, 42–0004—42–0231
—voting rights, 76–0019
Agassiz, L., 79–0021
Aged, institutions for, 74–0001
Agriculture, 33–0004; 40–0027; 42–0004—42–0231
Aguirre, Jose Maria de, 23–0002—23–4503; 23–5210; 51–0004—51–0125
Aguirre, R., 49–0001—49–0086
Ainsworth, W. G., 74–0019
Alabama Company, 23–0002—23–4503
Alaman, Lucas, 23–0002—23–4503
Alberry, Harvey, 23–0002—23–4503
Alcalde courts, 23–0002—23–4503
Alexander, Charles, 44–0006
Alexander, William, 22–0247; 49–0001—49–0086

Alexandria, Louisiana, 23–4920—23–4932
Allegheny, Pennsylvania, 70–0200—70–0418
Allen, Augustus C., 23–0002—23–4503; 35–0018—35–0122; 51–0004—
    51–0125
Allen, Charles C., 22–0247
Allen, Ebenezer, 23–0002—23–4503; 77–0003
Allen, F., 23–0002—23–4503
Allen, G. F., 04–0044
Allen, H. H., 23–0002—23–4503
Allen, Harriet E., 23–0002—23–4503
Allen, Henry R., 23–0002—23–4503
Allen, James M., 23–0002—23–4503
Allen, John K., 23–0002—23–4503
Allen, John Melville, 29–0028—29–0243; papers, 36–0003—36–0009
Allen, M. C., 23–0002—23–4503
Allen, Martin, 23–0002—23–4503
Allen, R., 23–0002—23–4503
Allen, Samuel L., 23–0002—23–4503
Allen, T. I., 23–0002—23–4503
Allen, William J., 29–0028—29–0243
Allen family, 23–0002—23–4503
Allen & Fulton, 23–0002—23–4503
Allen & Hale, 23–0002—23–4503
Almonte, Juan Nepomuceno, 23–0002—23–4503
Alsbury, Horace (Horatio), 70–1200—70–1258
Alta Loma, Texas, 78–0017
Alvey, J. P., 30–0850—30–0890; 79–0013
Alvin, Texas, 79–0015
Amanoale, Lorenzo, 28–0156—28–0170
American Building Maintenance Company, 79–0005
American Guild of Organists, Galveston Chapter, records, 76–0011
American Library Association, 79–0005
American party, 76–0037
American Power & Light Company, 56–0005
American Red Cross, Galveston Chapter, records, 19–0027
Amnesty law, Mexican, 23–0002—23–4503
Anaheim, California, 35–0018—35–0122
Anahuac, Texas, 23–0002—23–4503
Anderson, Alfred, 40–0027
Anderson, Caroline T. Gwyn, 40–0027
Anderson, Charles Harper, 40–0027
Anderson, E. H., 35–0018—35–0122
Anderson, Kenneth L., 29–0028—29–0243
Anderson, Mary Gwyn, 40–0027
Anderson, S. T. L., 40–0027
Anderson, Taliaferro, 40–0027
Anderson, Texas, 23–0002—23–4503; 70–0475—70–0492; 72–0524—72–
    1992
Anderson County, 78–0014

Andrews, Edmund, 23–0002—23–4503; 51–0004—51–0125
Andrews, Henrietta Lamar Calder, 35–0018—35–0122
Andrews, Henry B., 23–0002—23–4503; 70–1150—70–1178; 79–0005
Andrews, James, 70–0200—70–0418
Andrews, John, 23–0002—23–4503
Andrews, Richard, 23–0002—23–4503; 29–0028—29–0243
Andrews, Robert Henry, 51–0004—51–0125
Andrews, Stephen Pearl, 29–0028—29–0243
Andrews, Wright S., 23–0002—23–4503
Andrews & Sayre, 23–0002—23–4503
Angelina County, Texas, 56–0005; 78–0014
Angerhoffer, H. P., Mrs., 42–0232—42–0287
Angier, John, 23–4920—23–4932
Angle, G. W., 74–0019
Angleton, Texas, 79–0019
Anna Maria (Mexican schooner), 72–0001
Ansteadt, Joseph, 51–0004—51–0125
Anti-Defamation League, 78–0024
Arcadia, Texas, 56–0005
Archer, Branch Tanner, 23–0002—23–4503; 29–0028—29–0243
Architecture, 72–1995, 74–0004
Arciniego, Miguel, 23–0002—23–4503
Ardrey, James M., 79–0027
Ardrey & Sexton, 79–0027
Armstrong, Thaddeus C., papers, 40–0002—40–0015b
Armstrong, William T., 40–0002—40–0015b; 72–0524—72–1992
Armstrong, William, & Brother, 23–0002—23–4503
Army Transport Service, 78–0022
Arnett, Walter A., 77–0004
Artists, 73–0342. *See also* Organizations, art
Ash, Henry, 33–0041—33–0093
Ashton, William, 70–0100—70–0162
Ashton Villa, 74–0011
Astor House, New York, 23–0002—23–4503
Astoria, Oregon, 42–0232—42–0287
Atascosito, Texas, 23–0002—23–4503
Atchison, Topeka & Santa Fe Railway Company, 28–0233
Athens, Texas, 74–0019
Atkinson, Edward, 72–0524—72–1992
Atlanta, Georgia, 25–0553—25–0567
Auchincloss, James, 23–0002—23–4503
Audress, E. O., 78–0014
Augsburg, Germany, 36–1202
Augusta, Maine, 79–0029
Aury, Louis, 29–0028—29–0243
Austin (sloop), 23–0002—23–4503; 33–0001; 72–0001
Austin, Archibald, 23–0002—23–4503
Austin, Edward T., 22–0247; 23–0002—23–4503; 51–0004—51–0125; 69–0266—69–0273; 70–1150—70–1178

Austin, Eliza, 23–0002—23–4503
Austin, Huldah, 23–0002—23–4503
Austin, James Elijah Brown, 23–0002—23–4503
Austin, John, 23–0002—23–4503; 29–0028—29–0243; 51–0004—51–0125
Austin, Moses, 23–0002—23–4503; 29–0028—29–0243; 35–0018—35–0122
Austin, Stephen Fuller, 23–0002—23–4503; 29–0028—29–0243; 30–0850—30–0890; 50–0001; 79–0021
Austin, V. E., 76–0019
Austin, William Tennant, 23–0002—23–4503; 25–0525—25–0552; 29–0028—29–0243; 73–0055—73–0341
Austin, Texas, 22–0247; 23–0002—23–4503; 25–0525—25–0552; 30–0850—30–0890; 32–0008—32–0071; 36–0045—36–1201; 40–0002—40–0015b; 42–0004—42–0231; 70–0200—70–0418; 71–0376—71–0383; 71–0387; 72–0001; 72–0524—72–1992; 73–0055—73–0341; 74–0018; 75–0004; 79–0013; 79–0015; 79–0020
Austin & Butrand, 70–0100—70–0162
Austin & Edrington, 70–0100—70–0162
Austin & Rose, 78–0014
Austin City Gazette, 23–0002—23–4503
Austin County, Texas, 23–0002—23–4503; 36–1202; 78–0014
Austin Junior High School, 79–0015
Autographs, 25–0592; 28–0295; 34–0033; 76–0027; 79–0021
Ayers, Gardner & Company, 78–0014
Ayish Bayou, Texas, 23–0002—23–4503
Aziola Club, records, 25–0592

Bache, Louise F., 15–0001; 67–0021—67–0022
Bache, Professor———, 23–0002—23–4503
Bache, Richard, 29–0028—29–0243; 74–0018
Bacon, John, 29–0028—29–0243
Badgett quadruplets, 77–0005
Bagby, Thomas M., 72–0524—72–1992
Bailey, George H., 35–0018—35–0122
Bailey, John E., 79–0012
Bailey, Nathaniel, 70–0100—70–0162
Baird, Texas, 74–0019
Baker, J. R., 35–0018—35–0122
Baker, Moseley, 23–0002—23–4503; 29–0028—29–0243
Baker, O. T., 79–0020
Baker, Presley C., 79–0005; 79–0024
Baker, R. P., 70–0425—70–0474
Baker, Botts & Lovett, 75–0004
Baker settlement, 23–0002—23–4503
Baldwin, William H., & Company, 22–0247
Ball, Albert, 22–0153—22–0246; 23–0002—23–4503; 70–0100—70–0162; 73–0055—73–0341
Ball, George, 23–0002—23–4503; 72–1995; 79–0005
Ball, Munger T., 71–0386

Ball, Sarah C., 49–0001—49–0006; 52–0019—52–0023
Ball, A. & G., 23–0002—23–4503
Ball, Hutchings & Company, 23–0002—23–4503; 28–0233; 28–0037—28–0041; records, 49–0001—49–0006; 52–0019—52–0023; 73–0055—73–0341; 78–0014; 79–0012; 80–0001
Ballew, Page, 22–0247
Ballew, R. T., 72–0524—72–1992
Ballinger, Harriet P. ("Hallie"), 70–0475—70–0492
Ballinger, Lucy, 70–0475—70–0492
Ballinger, Thomas J., 78–0014
Ballinger, William Pitt, 22–0153—22–0246; 23–0002—23–4503; 28–0061—28–0101; 28–0233; 40–0002—40–0015b; papers, 50–0001; materials, 71–0326—71–0370; 72–0524—72–1992; 73–0055—73–0341; 79–0005
Ballinger, Mott & Terry, 28–0233
Ballinger & Jack, 23–0002—23–4503
Baltimore, Maryland, 22–0023; 23–0002—23–4503; 23–4920—23–4932; 23–4909—23–4919; 67–0080; 73–0055—73–0341; 74–0018
Baltimore & Frederick-Town Turnpike Road, 24–0088
Baltimore & Ohio Railroad, 23–0002—23–4503
Bangs, Samuel, 29–0028—29–0243
Bangs & Fletcher, 23–0002—23–4503
Banks, Edgar J., 78–0019
Banks and banking, 23–0002—23–4503; 40–0027; 44–0001; 49–0001—49–0006; 52–0019—52–0023; 72–1994; 77–0004; 78–0009; 78–0025; 78–0027; 79–0013; 80–0001—80–0003
Baptist church, 41–0002—41–0005; 72–1995; 78–0014; 79–0000
Barbour County, Alabama, 22–0247
Barnes, S. W., 29–0028—29–0243
Barnes, Thomas, 36–0045—36–1201
Barnstone, Howard, 71–0192—71–0195
Barnum, P. T., 79–0021
Baron, J. A., 73–0055—73–0341
Barr, Robert, 23–0002—23–4503
Barre, Nicholas, 30–0850—30–0890
Barrett, Don Carlos, 23–0002—23–4503; 29–0028—29–0243
Barry, Bryan T., 70–0200—70–0418
Barry, James B., 29–0028—29–0242
Barton, A. M., 29–0028—29–0242
Barton, Clara, 28–0295
Barton, S. M., & Company, 22–0247
Barttell, T., 72–0524—72–1992
Bastrop, Felipe Enrique Neri Baron de, 23–0002—23–4503; 29–0028—29–0243
Bastrop, Texas, 23–0002—23–4503; 33–0041—33–0093; 72–0524—72–1992; 73–0055—73–0341
Bateman, Simeon, 29–0028—29–0243
Bates, Joseph, 23–0002—23–4503; 73–0055—73–0341
Batesville, Texas, 35–0018—35–0122; 74–0019

Baton Rouge, Louisiana, 32–0008—32–0071; 71–0386; 72–0524—72–1992
Battle Creek, Michigan, 79–0019
Baudoux, Marcel, & Company, 70–1287
Bauer, William H., 71–0386
Baugh, G. E., 74–0019
Baugh, O. T., 74–0019
Bautsch, Amalia, 79–0011
Bayless, W. F., 79–0014
Baylor, George Wythe, 29–0028—29–0243
Baylor, John R., 29–0028—29–0243
Baylor, Lucie C., 22–0023
Beach Club, 46–0002
Beach Hotel & Seaside Improvement Company, records, 30–0956—30–0991
Beale, Elizabeth A., 72–0524—72–1992
Beales, John Charles, 23–0002—23–4503; 29–0028—29–0243
Bean, Aaron, 22–0247
Bean, B. F., 77–0004
Bean, Colonel———, 35–0018—35–0122
Bean, Louisa, 22–0247
Bean, Maria, 22–0247
Bean, Peter Ellis, 29–0028—29–0243
Bean's Wharf, 22–0247
Beard, J. S., 36–0045—36–1201
Beasley Michael, 73–0055—73–0341
Beaty, George, 72–0001
Beau & Routier & Marseille, 30–0998
Beaumont, Texas, 23–0002—23–4503; 35–0018—35–0122; 70–0100—70–0162; 71–0386; 73–0055—73–0341; 79–0015; 79–0019
Beauregard, P. G. T., 79–0021
Beck, Thomas W., 36–0045—36–1201
Becker, August C., 78–0014
Bee, Bernard E., 23–0002—23–4503; 29–0028—29–0243
Beecher, H. W., 79–0021
Beech Grove, Tennessee, 25–0553—25–0567
Beers, Iola Barnes, 36–0045—36–1201
Beers, Jonathan Sturges, 23–0002—23–4503; 36–0045—36–1201
Beers, Joseph D., 23–0002—23–4503
Beers, William Francis, 36–0045—36–1201
Beers, Mrs. William Francis, 52–0123
Beers, Kennison & Company, 36–0045—36–1201
Beers, St. John & Company, 23–0002—23–4503
Beers family, papers, 36–0045—36–1201
Beers & Prevost, 36–0045—36–1201
Beissner, Charles L., papers, 77–0004; 78–0014; 78–0025; 78–0027
Beissner, George W., 77–0004
Beissner, Henry, 22–0247
Beissner, Louise, 77–0004
Belknap, Ray H., 78–0017

Bell, Daniel W., 22–0247
Bell, Josiah Hughes, 23–0002—23–4503; 70–0475—70–0492
Bell, P. Hansborough, 23–0002—23–4503
Bell & Brothers, 22–0247
Bell County, Texas, 78–0014; 78–0017
Belleste, M. Seminaro de, 29–0028—29–0243
Bellville, Texas, 23–0002—23–4503; 67–0080
Belo, Alfred Horatio, 70–0200—70–0418
Belton, Texas, 23–0002—23–4503; 28–0233; 51–0004—51–0125; 76–0016
Beltran, Jose Maria, 23–0002—23–4503
Benjamin, I. P., 79–0021
Benner, Andrew, 51–0004—51–0125
Bennet, Joseph L., 29–0028—29–0243
Bennet, Miles Squire, 29–0028—29–0243
Bennet, Valentine, 29–0028—29–0243; 35–0018—35–0122
Bennett, E. B., 27–0044—27–0699
Bennett, Harry, papers, 42–0232—42–0287
Bennett, Theodore, 67–0080
Benton, Thomas H., 79–0021
Beramendi, Juan Martin de, 23–0002—23–4503
Berkemeier, F., 56–0005
Berlin, Germany, 22–0023
Berlocher, John, 22–0247; 23–0002—23–4503
Bernard, Joseph H., 29–0028—29–0242
Berry, Andrew Jackson, 29–0028—29–0242
Berry, J. T., 74–0019
Bexar, Texas, 23–0002—23–4503
Bexar County, Texas, 78–0014
Bianchine, Rafael, 28–0293
Bicycling, 78–0025
Biddle, Nicholas, 23–0002—23–4503
Biering, E. J., 77–0004
Billings, Josh, 79–0021
Billups, G. R., 70–1200—70–1258
Bippert, John, 74–0019
Biscoe, W. S. A., 70–1150—70–1178
Bishop, E. B., 28–0061—28–0101
Bismarck, Prince Otto Edward Leopold von, 28–0295
Bissig, J. W., 79–0011
Black, W. C., 72–0524—72–1992
"Black bean" episode, 72–0102—72–0103
Blacksmithing, 23–0002—23–4503
Blagden, John D., 46–0006
Blagge, Henry W., 28–0102—28–0128
Blaine, Harriet S., 24–0088
Blaine, James G., 24–0088
Blakely, Fannie E., 78–0019
Blanco, Victor, 23–0002—23–4503
Blaylock, L. W., 29–0028—29–0243

Bleicke, William, 22–0247
Block, Alice, 52–0123
Bloodgood, M., 22–0247
Bloodgood, William, 22–0247; 23–0002—23–4503
Blount, Stephen W., 29–0028—29–0243
Blum, Leon, 56–0005
Blum, Leon & H., Land Company, 56–0005; 78–0014
B'Nai Israel Temple, 79–0033
Bohmken, H., 79–0011
Bohn, Nic, 76–0019
Bolivar Peninsula, 23–0002—23–4503
Bolivar Point, 30–0200
Bolling, E. S., 23–4971—23–4993
Bolton, Herbert E., 35–0018—35–0122
Bonaparte, Louis-Napoleon, 24–0088; 79–0021
Bond family, papers, 79–0016
Bondies, George, 78–0014
Bondies, W., 22–0023
Bonham, Louisiana, 36–0045—36–1201
Bonnell, George W., 29–0028—29–0243
Bonnell, Will H., 74–0019
Booth, Edwin, 79–0021
Booth, William L., 72–0524—72–1992
Bordeaux, France, 69–0274
Borden, Gail, Jr., 23–0002—23–4503; papers, 25–0001—25–0521; 27–0041;
        29–0028—29–0243; 35–0018—35–0122; 46–0002; 51–0004—51–
        0125; 72–0001; 74–0018; 77–0013; 79–0000
Borden, John G., 25–0001—25–0521
Borden, John Pettit, 23–0002—23–4503; 51–0004—51–0125
Borden, Paschal P., 23–0002—23–4503; 25–0001—25–0521
Borden, Thomas Henry, 23–0002—23–4503; 25–0001—25–0521; 51–
        0004—51–0125
Bordon & Bordon Live Stock Company, 78–0014
Bosque County, Texas, 22–0247; 36–0045—36–1201
Bostick, Sion R., 29–0028—29–0243
Boston, Massachusetts, 23–0002—23–4503
Boston Times, 72–0001
Bostwick, John R. R. and Helen C., 73–0055—73–0341
Botts, Benjamin A., 72–0524—72–1992
Botts, W. B., 69–0266—69–0273
Bowen, M. C., 76–0019
Bowen, R. D., 28–0293
Bowie, James, 23–0002—23–4503; 29–0028—29–0242
Bowles, Benjamin, 23–0002—23–4503; 29–0028—29–0243
Bowyer, Otis and John, 74–0019
Boydton, Virginia, 22–0057—22–0152
Bradberry vs. *Williams et al.*, 23–0002—23–4503
Bradburn, Juan Davis, 23–0002—23–4503; 29–0028—29–0243
Bradbury, D., papers, 33–0021—33–0023; 70–0100—70–0162

Bradley, William, 62–0001
Bradshaw, Velma, 79–0020
Brady, Frank, 78–0014
Brady, Texas, 78–0017
Bragg, Braxton, papers, 32–0008
Bragg, Dunbar, 32–0008
Branard, George A., diary, 40–0016
Branch, A. W., 22–0057—22–0152
Branch, Anthony Martin, 29–0028—29–0243
Brannum, William, 72–0001
Brashear, William C., 72–0001
Brauch, Wharton, 79–0019
Brazil, 69–0005—69–0050
Brazoria (schooner), 23–0002—23–4503
Brazoria County, Texas, 22–0247; 23–0002—23–4503; 56–0005; 69–0274;
    70–0162; 70–0475—70–0492; 70–1179—70–1189; 73–0055—73–
    0341; 78–0014
Brazos County, Texas, 22–0247
Brazos Railroad, 74–0018
Brazos River, 23–0002—23–4503; 70–0100—70–0162
Brazos Santiago, Texas, 74–0018
Breckinridge, Clifton R., 70–0200—70–0418
Bremen, Germany, 23–0002—23–4503; 36–1202; 42–0232—42–0287; 79–
    0011
Brenham, Richard F., 29–0028—29–0243
Brenham, Texas, 23–0002—23–4503; 27–0044—27–0699; 28–0233; 30–
    0197; 31–1191—31–1194; 32–0008; 42–0004—42–0231; 51–0004—
    51–0125; 70–0200—70–0418; 70–1150—70–1178; 72–0524—72–
    1992; 73–0055—73–0341
Brewster, Edward, 23–0002—23–4503
Brewster, Henry Percy, 29–0028—29–0243
Brewster, Robert, 22–0247; 23–0002—23–4503
Briggs, Annie Wood, 79–0010
Briggs, George W., 29–0028—29–0243
Briggs, Jacob L., 22–0247; 23–0002—23–4503; 28–0293; 70–0425—70–
    0474
Briggs & Yard, 23–0002—23–4503
Brigham, Asa, 72–0001
Brin, Sam, 77–0004
Brindley, Anne, 79–0020
Bringhurst, Nettie Houston, 35–0018—35–0122
Briscoe, Andrew, 29–0028—29–0243
British consulate, Galveston, 1846–50, 49–0007—49–0013
Broadsides, 30–0197; 76–0019
Brockelman, Joseph, 79–0014
Brooks, B. E., 36–0045—36–1201
Brooks, John Towers, 29–0028—29–0243
Brooks, William, 36–0045—36–1201
Brown, Augustus I., 71–0385

Brown, Dunn, 28–0293
Brown, Estel Park, 56–0005
Brown, Frank, 73–0055—73–0341
Brown, Henry S., 23–0002—23–4503; 29–0028—29–0243
Brown, J. M., 23–0002—23–4503; 72–1995; 74–0011
Brown, Jeremiah, 23–0002—23–4503; 72–0001
Brown, John C., 70–0200—70–0418
Brown, John Henry, 29–0028—29–0243
Brown, Joseph S., 42–0232—42–0287
Brown, Reuben R., 29–0028—29–0243
Brown, Robert A., 76–0038
Brown, Cherry & Wilson, 77–0004
Brown, J. S., Hardware Company, 78–0014
Brown, Lane & Jackson, 78–0014
Brown County, Texas, 56–0005
Browne, Samuel P., 23–0002—23–4503
Brownsville, Texas, 23–0002—23–4503; 33–0041—33–0093; 69–0274; 71–0386
Brownwood, Texas, 74–0019
Bruer, Thomas D., 80–0010
Brunswich, Germany, 36–1202
Brutus (ship), 23–0002—23–4503; 72–0001
Bryan, Guy Morrison, 23–0002—23–4503; 29–0028—29–0243; 51–0004—51–0125; 70–0475—70–0492
Bryan, J. P., 73–0055—73–0341
Bryan, John Neely, 35–0018—35–0122
Bryan, Laura H. ("Jack"), 70–0475—70–0492
Bryan, Moses Austin, 23–0002—23–4503; 29–0028—29–0243; 51–0004—51–0125
Bryan, William, 23–0002—23–4503; 36–0045—36–1201
Bryan, William Joel, 23–0002—23–4503; 29–0028—29–0243
Bryan, Texas, 22–0247, 23–0002—23–4503; 33–0041—33–0093
Bryant, C. G., 70–0425—70–0474; 72–1995
Bryant, J. P., 73–0055—73–0341
Brynum, Texas, 67–0080
Buchanan, James, 79–0021
Buckingham, Virginia, 22–0247
Buckley, Daniel J., 28–0061—28–0101; 79–0008
Buckley, Edward, 74–0010
Buckley, Henry, 28–0102—28–0128
Buckner, Aylett C., 23–0002—23–4503; 29–0028—29–0243
Buffalo Bayou, 23–0002—23–4503
Buffalo Bayou, Brazos & Colorado Railway Company, 74–0018
Buffalo Bluff, Florida, 22–0247
Bulloch, Letticia M., 22–0247
Bunker, Thomas C., 22–0153—22–0246
Bunnemeyer, B., 29–0028—29–0243
Bunting, Dr. and Mrs. R. F., 25–0553—25–0567; 77–0004
Burial records. *See* Death and burial records

Burleson, Albert Sidney, 75–0004
Burleson, Edward, Sr., 23–0002—23–4503; 29–0028—29–0243; 79–0021
Burleson, Edward, Jr., 29–0028—29–0243
Burleson, James, 23–0002—23–4503; 79–0027
Burleson, Rufus Columbus, 23–0002—23–4503; 29–0028—29–0243
Burnam, Jesse, 29–0028—29–0243
Burnet, David Gouverneur, 23–0002—23–4503; 25–0525—23–0552; papers, 26–0004—26–0353; 31–0001—31–1096; 31–1231—31–1243; 72–0001
Burnet, Texas, 71–0376—71–0383
Burnham, James G., 25–0001—25–0521
Burnley, Albert Triplett, 23–0002—23–4503; 29–0028—29–0243
Burnley, Susan G., 22–0023
Burns, James A., 51–0004—51–0125
Burr, Seth, 70–1179—70–1189
Burress, Mrs. Walter M., 62–0003—62–0200
Burroughs, J. M., 04–0049—04–0050
Burton, Isaac Watts, 72–0001
Burton, Margaret Sealy, autograph collection, 28–0295
Burton, Texas, 22–0247; 28–0055—28–0060
Bush, N. W., 73–0055—73–0341
Bush, S. D., 28–0293
Bushnell, Horace, 04–0001—04–0007
Busselle, J. T., 77–0004
Bustamante, Anastacio, 23–0002—23–4503
Butler, Anthony, 23–0002—23–4503
Butler, E. B. M., 32–0008
Butler & Ballinger, 23–0002—23–4503
Buttlar, August, 14–0030
Byne, W. H., 72–0524—72–1992

Cabeza de Vaca, Alvar Nunez, 29–0028—29–0243
Cade, C. T., 75–0004
Caduc, P. J., 23–0002—23–4503
Cagle, J. F., 77–0004
Cahill Cemetery, records, 77–0033
Caldwell, Matthew, 29–0028—29–0243
Caldwell & Walker, 26–0372—26–0375; 27–0033—27–0039
Calhoun, John C., 79–0021
Calhoun County, Texas, 56–0005
California, 23–0002—23–4503; gold rush in, 40–0002—40–0015b
California Insurance Company, 78–0017
Callahan, James Hughes, 29–0028—29–0243
Calvert, Robert, 72–0524—72–1992
Calvert, Texas, 22–0247
Cameron, Ewen, 29–0028—29–0243
Cameron, J. C., 68–0143—69–0147
Cameron, John, 23–0002—23–4503; 29–0028—29–0243
Cameron, Texas, 23–0002—23–4503; 27–0044—27–0699

Campbell, A. R., 78–0014
Campbell, Andrew Monroe, 79–0029
Campbell, Dr. [?], 23–0002—23–4503; 73–0055—73–0341
Campbell, James, 29–0028—29–0243
Campbell, Robert C., 23–0002—23–4503; 25–0525—25–0552
Campbell, Victoria Williams, 79–0029
Campbell & Rickerly, 36–0045—36–1201
Campbell-Fuller papers, 79–0029
Campbellton, Texas, 74–0019
Camp Colorado, Texas, 74–0019
Camp Hunter, Louisiana, 23–4920—23–4932
Camp Magruder, Louisiana, 55–0001
Canals, 33–0014—33–0020; 71–0386
Caney, Texas, 22–0153—22–0246
Canfield, Alanson M., 51–0004—51–0125
Canon, R. B., 74–0019
Carbajal, Jose Maria Jesus, 23–0002—23–4503
Carnes, James E., 29–0028—29–0243
Carnes, William C., 28–0293
Carr, William, 51–0004—51–0125
Carrico, Marcy W., 74–0010
Carruth, E. B., 35–0018—35–0122
Carruthers, W. S., 78–0014
Carson, Samuel P., 29–0028—29–0243
Carter, George W., 25–0525—25–0552
Carter, J. W., 27–0044—27–0699
Cartoons, political, 76–0044
Cassin, William, 74–0019
Castleton, Vermont, 77–0003
Castro, Henri, 29–0028—29–0242
Castroville, Texas, 36–1202; 74–0019
Catholic church. *See* Roman Catholic church
Catonsville, Maryland, 23–4909—23–4919
Cattle raising, 23–0002—23–4503
Cauley, R. H. S., 72–0524—72–1992
Cave, Eber Worthington, 29–0028—29–0243
Cayce, H. P., 30–0850—30–0890
Cazneau, William Leslie, 23–0002—23–4503; 29–0028—29–0243
Cecil, Benedict, 73–0055—73–0341
Cedar Point (Houston's home), 23–0002—23–4503
Cemeteries, 71–0207
Census, scholastic, 78–0018
Centerville, Texas, 72–0524—72–1992
Central Transit Railway, 22–0247
Centre on the Strand, 72–1995; 74–0010; records, 75–0008
Chambers, Thomas Jefferson, 23–0002—23–4503; 29–0028—29–0243; 79–0019
"Champ d'Asile," 27–0041; article, 47–0002
Chapman, I. H. F., 22–0247

Chappell Hill, Texas, 23–0002—23–4503; 30–0197; 42–0004—42–0231
Charleston, South Carolina, 22–0023; 23–0002—23–4503
Charlottesville, Virginia, 22–0023; 23–0002—23–4503
Chataignon, Marius S., papers, 72–1993
Chauldron, Jean Simon, letters, 47–0001
Cheatham, Benjamin F., 25–0553—25–0567
Cheesborough, Edmund Reed, papers, 22–0024; 56–0005
Cherry, Wilbur F., 72–1995
Chiapas Corporation, 78–0019
Chicago, Illinois, 70–0200—70–0418
Children, 40–0027; 78–0021; 79–0005
Childress, George Campbell, 29–0028—29–0243
Childs, Dr. Samuel R., 79–0021
Chilton, Horace, 75–0004
China, sale of arms to, 44–0002—44–0005
Chittenden, Larry, 79–0021
Chocolate Bayou, Texas, 23–0002—23–4503; 70–0475—70–0492
Cholera, 22–0009—22–0021; 23–0002—23–4503
Chriesman, Horatio, 23–0002—23–4503; 29–0028—29–0243
Christiansen, James, 56–0005
Christie, B. Y., & Company, 78–0019
Christy, William H., 23–0002—23–4503; 36–0003—36–0009
Chubb, Phoebe, 73–0055—73–0341
Chubb, Thomas H., 23–0002—23–4503; 53–0001; 70–0100—70–0162; 73–0055—73–0341
Church of Mexico, 23–0002—23–4503
Cincinnati, Ohio, 04–0001—04–0007; 23–0002—23–4503
Cinelli, Angelo, 77–0004
Cistern, Texas, 79–0014
Citizen's State Bank of Texas City, 40–0027
Civil War, 04–0044; 10–0001; 23–4920—23–4932; 24–0007—24–0035; 25–0525—25–0552; 25–0553—25–0567; 27–0019—27–0022; 27–0701; 30–0197; 31–1180—31–1183; 31–1191—31–1194; 32–0008; 33–0021—33–0023; 33–0097; 35–0018—35–0122; 36–0041; 36–0045—36–1201; 40–0002—40–0015b; 40–0016; 42–0004—42–0231; 44–0007; 44–0008—44–0015; 50–0001; 51–0004—51–0125; 51–0126; 53–0001; 55–0001; 69–0005—69–0050; 70–0475—70–0492; 70–1150—70–1178; 71–0326—71–0370; 71–0376—71–0393; 72–0524—72–1992; 74–0010; 74–0018; 75–0001—75–0001a; scrapbooks, 76–0041; 77–0002; 77–0011
Clardy, Arthur, 78–0017
Clark, Edward, 25–0525—25–0552
Clark, Mrs. Robert, 77–0004
Clark, Stedman, 22–0247
Clark, Thomas Holmes, 22–0247
Clark, Fletcher & Company, 22–0247
Clarke & Courts, 78–0014
Clarke County, Alabama, 42–0004—42–0231
Clary, M. P., 72–0524—72–1992

Clason & Company, 30–0998
Clay, Nestor, 23–0002—23–4503; 29–0028—29–0243
Clayton, Nicholas Joseph, 27–0044—27–0699; 72–1995; papers, 74–0004;
    78–0014
Clayton, N. J., & Company, 79–0008
Clayton & Lynch, 74–0004
Cleburne, Patrick N., 25–0553—25–0567
Cleburne, Texas, 27–0044—27–0699; 28–0233; 50–0308—50–0357
Clemens, Jeremiah, 29–0028—29–0243
Clement & Dwyer, 23–0002—23–4503; 70–0100—70–0162
Cleveland, C. L., 70–0200—70–0418
Cleveland, J. Stewart, 74–0019
Cleveland, Jesse A. H., 23–4971—23–4993; 51–0004—51–0125
Cleveland, William D., 70–0200—70–0418; 74–0019
Clifford, Charles G., 29–0028—29–0243
Clingman, J. I., 77–0004
Coahuila and Texas, 23–0002—23–4503; laws and decrees, 23–5210
Coastal zone management, 78–0024
Coast Artillery Company, 127th, papers, 77–0030
Coates, John, 22–0247
Cobb, H. A., 23–0002—23–4503; 36–0003—36–0009
Cobb, Howell, 25–0553—25–0567
Cocke, James, 23–0002—23–4503; 70–0425—70–0474
Cockrell, F. M., 79–0021
Cocks, James, 72–0524—72–1992
Coddington, Eleanor, 78–0019
Coeler, Caroline, 30–0998
Cohen, Henry, papers, 79–0033
Coke, Richard, 70–0200—70–0418; 79–0021
Colbert, John W., 74–0019
Colbow, Walter, 72–0524—72–1992
Cold Springs, Texas, 23–0002—23–4503; 79–0019
Cole, Hugh L., 32–0008
Cole, J. P., 69–0266—69–0273
Cole, James P., 70–0425—70–0474
Coleman, M. E., 22–0023
Coleman, Robert N., 29–0028—29–0243
Coleman County, Texas, 78–0014
Colfax, Sayler, 79–0021
Collingsworth, James F., 23–0002—23–4503; 29–0028—29–0243
Collins, James P., 23–0002—23–4503; 73–0055—73–0341
Collins, Joseph, letter, 44–0019
Colombo, LeRoy, 81–0001
Colonization, 23–0002—23–4503
Colorado (ship), 72–0001
Colorado County, 23–0002—23–4503
Colorado Navigation Company, 23–0002—23–4503
Colorado Railroad, 74–0018
Colorado River, 23–0002—23–4503

110

Columbia, Pennsylvania, 32–0008
Columbia, Texas. *See* West Columbia, Texas
Columbus, Texas, 22–0247; 23–0002—23–4503; 42–0004—42–0231; 73–0055—73–0341; 79–0011; 79–0026
Comal County, Texas, 78–0014
Comal Manufacturing Company, 56–0005
Comanche, Texas, 27–0044—27–0699
Comanche (steamer), 23–0002—23–4503. See also *Cumanche*
Comanche Indians, 23–0002—23–4503
Commercial treaty, 23–0002—23–4503
Commission merchants, 56–0005; 69–0005—69–0050; 72–0524—72–1992; 79–0004—79–0029
Committee for Pier 19, records, 79–0037
Committee for the Defense of Galveston Island, 30–0849
Committee of 500, 56–0005
Compton, A. G., 23–0002—23–4503; 73–0055—73–0341
Compton, Thomas E., 24–0007—24–0035
Compton manuscript, 29–0244
Concho County, Texas, 78–0014
Concordia Society, 77–0004
Confederate States of America: military orders, 10–0001; 36–0041; 40–0016; 44–0008—44–0015; navy, 53–0001; 55–0001; army, 69–0005—69–0050
Conkling, Roscoe, 79–0021
Consolidated Metal Company, 78–0022
Content, Texas, 25–0525—25–0552
Contraband, 44–0002—44–0005
Convict labor contracts, 28–0037—28–0041
Cook, Francis, 25–0001—25–0521
Cook, William M., 23–0002—23–4503; 23–4902—23–4908; 70–1200—70–1258
Cooke, Charles, 22–0247
Cooke, Louis B., 29–0028—29–0243
Cooke, Louis P., 72–0001
Cooke, William F., 23–4920—23–4932
Cooke, William G., 23–0002—23–4503; 29–0028—29–0243
Cooper, Agnes, 79–0019
Cooper, Bayliss P., Jr., 79–0019
Cooper, Bayliss P., papers, 79–0019
Cooper, Eliza, 79–0019
Cooper, Francis De Lancy, 79–0019
Cooper, S. B., 75–0004
Cooper, W. A., 74–0019
Copano, Texas, 70–0100—70–0162
Corlis, James, 22–0247
Corly, J. Vernon, 22–0057—22–0152
Corpus Christi, Texas, 23–0002—23–4503; 70–0100—70–0162
Corsicana, Texas, 36–0045—36–1201; 70–0200—70–0418; 72–0524—72–1992; 79–0014

Cultural affairs, 75–0017; 76–0017; 76–0018
Cumanche (ship), 33–0097
Cummings, C. R., & Company, 79–0019
Cunningham, Bob, 79–0020
Cunningham, J. L., 74–0019
Cunningham, John R., 79–0019
Cunningham, W. S., 78–0014
Currie, James, 36–0045—36–1201
Currie, William, 36–0045—36–1201
Curtis, Edwin A., 27–0044—27–0699
Cusham, Charlotte, 79–0021
Cushing, Edward Hopkins, 29–0028—29–0243
Cushing, James S., 25–0001—25–0521
Customs collections, 23–0002—23–4503; 77–0013

Dabney, R. L., 22–0023
Dahill, Edward F., 79–0011
Dahl, Oliver, 28–0005—28–0036
Dailey, Fred B., 22–0247
Dainish, Antonio, 23–0002—23–4503
Daley, J. F., 79–0014
Dallas, George M., 27–0006—27–0012
Dallas, Texas, 76–0016
Dallas County, 24–0088; 56–0005; 70–0200—70–0418; 72–0524—72–1992;
    78–0014; 79–0019
Dallas News, 24–0088
Dallas Public University, 79–0005
Dalton, Georgia, 25–0553—25–0567
Damon, Texas, 79–0015
Danbury, Connecticut, 22–0023
Dancy, John Winfield Scott, 29–0028—29–0243
Daniel, Charles, 23–0002—23–4503; 73–0055—73–0341
Daniel, Price, 71–0387
Daniels, Joseph, 29–0028—29–0243
Danzey, B., 72–0524—72–1992
Daran, William P., 31–1191—31–1194
Darden, Stephen Heard, 29–0028—29–0242; 35–0018—35–0122
Darling, Timothy, 25–0001—25–0521
Darlington, John Washington, 29–0028—29–0243
Darlington, Maryland, 23–4909—23–4919
Darragh, John L., papers, 27–0044—27–0699; 27–0702; 52–0122; 72–1995;
    79–0019
Darst & Wallace, 23–0002—23–4503
Dashiell, Jeremiah Yellott, papers, 10–0001
Daugherty, Jacamiah Seaman, 74–0019
Daughters of the Confederacy. *See* United Daughters of the Confederacy
Davenport, Cora, 40–0027
Davenport, Harris, 40–0027
Davenport, Samuel, 29–0028—29–0243

Davidson, H. P., 19–0027
Davidson, R. V., 78–0014
Davidson, W. R., 74–0019
Davidson, Minor & Hawkins, 78–0014
Davidson & Jack, 78–0017
Davidson & Minor, 78–0014
Davie, John P., 23–0002—23–4503; 28–0005—28–0036
Davie, J. P., & Company, records, 79–0004; 79–0008
Davis, B. H., 70–0200—70–0418
Davis, B. R., 28–0102—28–0128
Davis, Bevia R., 22–0247
Davis, Biddy, 73–0055—73–0341
Davis, De Will C., 74–0019
Davis, Edmund Jackson, letters, 31–1191—31–1194
Davis, Eugene, 74–0019
Davis, J. J., 73–0055—73–0341
Davis, Jack, 73–0055—73–0341
Davis, Jefferson, 44–0002—44–0005; 79–0021
Davis, John A., 70–0425—70–0474
Davis, Samuel, 22–0247
Davis, Sarah H., 29–0028—29–0243
Davis, Waters S., papers, 24–0068—24–0070; 78–0017
Davis, S. S., & Company, bankers, 23–0002—23–4503
Davison Company, 78–0014
Dawson, Nicholas Mosby, 29–0028—29–0243
Day, Julia Ann, 75–0005
Dean, John, 23–0002—23–4503; 70–1150—70–1178
Death and burial records, 14–0030; 28–0293; 52–0019—52–0023; 52–
    0030—52–0121; 71–0390; 79–0035; 79–0036
Deats, James K., 79–0014
DeBruhl, John, 22–0247
DeCordova, Jacob, 70–0100—70–0162; 73–0055—73–0341
DeCordova & Sons, 74–0019
Delaware College, 23–0002—23–4503; 23–4920—23–4932
De Leon, Martin, 23–0002—23–4503; 29–0028—29–0243
Delesdenier, George H., 23–0002—23–4503; 51–0004—51–0125
Delispine, J. P., 70–0100—70–0162
De Morse, Charles, 29–0028—29–0243
DeNormandie, E., 78–0014
Dent, George R., 36–0045—36–1201
Dentistry, 23–0002—23–4503
Denton, John B., 23–0002—23–4503; 29–0028—29–0243; 35–0018—35–
    0122
Denton, Lane, 78–0023
Denton, R. D., 78–0009
Denton County, Texas, 22–0247; 78–0014
Denver, Colorado, 28–0293
Deshone, G. Gould, 70–0425—70–0474
Desmeth, H., 72–0524—72–1992

114

Desoto City, Mississippi, 42–0004—42–0231
Dewberry, John, 70–1150—70–1178
DeWitt, Green C., 23–0002—23–4503; 29–0028—29–0243
DeWitt County, Texas, 22–0247
Dewitt's Colony, 23–0002—23–4503
Dexter, Michigan, 36–0045—36–1201
DeYoung, John, 51–0004—51–0125
Diary of a Union Soldier, 77–0002
Diaz, Porfirio, 28–0295; 79–0021
Dickinson, Almazon, 29–0028—29–0243
Dickinson Bayou, 23–0002—23–4503; 74–0018
Dickinson Land Company, 78–0014
Dickinson Public Library, 79–0005
Dieckman, Christian Frederick Andreas, 23–0002—23–4503; 28–0005—
    28–0036; 78–0009
Dieckmann, Wilhelmine, 28–0005—28–0036
Dienst, Alex, 29–0028—29–0243
Dietzel, Auguste, 22–0247
Dikeman, Cyrus, 72–0524—72–1992
Dillard, H. M., 74–0019
Dillard, John, 72–0524—72–1992
Dimitt, Philip, 23–0002—23–4503; 29–0028—29–0243
Dimon, M. O., 73–0055—73–0341
Dirks, Albert, 78–0014
Dirks, Lenhart, 23–0002—23–4503; 73–0055—73–0341
Dirks, Theresa, 73–0055—73–0341
Dirty Thirty, 78–0023; 78–0024
District Court of Galveston County Record of Jury Certificates, 30–0849
Divescovi, Pietro, 72–0001
Dobbin, Leonard, 70–1200—70–1258
Dobbins, Archibald S., papers, 69–0005—69–0050
Dobbins, Pleasants & Company, 69–0005—69–0050
Dobbins First Arkansas Cavalry Brigade, 69–0005—69–0050
Dobie, J. Frank, 62–0003—62–0200
Dobie, Sterling, 72–0524—72–1992
Dodson, Archelaus Bynum, 29–0028—29–0243
Dodsworth, William, 22–0153—22–0246
Dollar Bay Fig Corporation, 78–0022
Donaldson, William, 36–0045—36–1201
Donelson, Andrew Jackson, 29–0028—29–0243
Donnell, W. D., 78–0014
Doran, John, 51–0004—51–0125
Dorau, W. P., 35–0018—35–0122
Dorsett, T. M., 79–0005
Dorsey, C. H., 24–0148—24–0151
Dorsey, Dr. J. G., 78–0017
Doss Brothers, 77–0004
Double Bayou, Texas, 22–0023
Douglas, William M., 70–0200—70–0418

Douglass, Richard, 72–0524—72–1992
Doyle, A. Conan, 28–0295
Dredging, 75–0016
Dreiss, Thompson & Company, 79–0014
Drewa, Ed F., 76–0019
Dreyfus, A. Stanley, 19–0027; article, 71–0207
Driscoll, W. C., 72–0524—72–1992
Dri-Steam Valve Corporation, 56–0005
Druggists, 22–0057—22–0152; 30–0997; 76–0001; 79–0014
Ducie, D. W., 79–0014
Dudley, T. W., 72–0524—72–1992
Duke, Thomas M., 23–0002—23–4503; 29–0028—29–0243
Duncan, James Cannon, 29–0028—29–0243
Dunkin, Thomas, 74–0019
Dunlap, Fannie M., 29–0028—29–0243
Dunlap, Richard G., 23–0002—23–4503
Dunn, John, family, 30–0892
Duran, W. P., 79–0021
Durnett, Samuel S., 71–0385
Durst, John, 23–0002—23–4503; 29–0028—29–0243; 35–0018—35–0122
Duval, Burr H., 29–0028—29–0243
Duval, John Crittenden, 29–0028—29–0243; 72–0524—72–1992; 74–0019
Duval, Thomas H., 23–0002—23–4503; 29–0028—29–0243
Duval, William P., 29–0028—29–0243
Dyer, Babette, 27–0006—27–0012
Dyer, Frances, 27–0006—27–0012
Dyer, John, 23–0002—23–4503; 27–0006—27–0012
Dyer, Joseph Osterman, papers, 79–0017
Dyer, Leon, 27–0006—27–0012
Dyer, Beers & Kenison, 36–0045—36–1201
Dykes, George M., 78–0019

Eads, James B., 28–0061—28–0101; 70–0200—70–0418
Eagle Grove, Texas, 42–0004—42–0231
Eagle Pass, Texas, 40–0002—40–0015
Eagles, Order of, 30–0896
Eakins, J. H., 78–0014
Earle, Samuel L., 70–1150—70–1178
Eastern Star, Order of, 77–0003
Eastham, Delha, 77–0004
Eastland, William M., 29–0028—29–0243
Eastman, Lewis M., 23–4920—23–4932
Eaton, Benjamin, 23–0002—23–4503; 28–0293; papers, 52–0122
Echer, W. A., 19–0027
Ector, M. D., 29–0028—29–0243
Edgar, Tom, 29–0028—29–0243
Edmondson, James, 70–0100—70–0162
Edmondson, Thomas, 23–0002—23–4503; 73–0055—73–0341
Edmunds, George Franklin, 79–0021

Edrington, James F., 70–0100—70–0162
Education, 23–0002—23–4503; 28–0293; 35–0018—35–0122; 71–0385; 76–0032; 78–0018; 79–0034; 81–0007. *See also* Galveston Independent School District
Edwards, Hayden, 29–0028—29–0243
Edwards, Monroe, 23–0002—23–4503; 29–0028—29–0243
Ehrenberg, Herman, 29–0028—29–0243
Eiband's, 78–0017
Eichkorst, Richard, 79–0019
Eilers, Louis, 23–0002—23–4503
Eisenhour, Virginia, 65–0008
Eldridge, John C., 72–0524—72–1992
Eldridge, Joseph C., 29–0028—29–0243
Elections, 23–0002—23–4503
Elite Cafe, 77–0003
Elliot, Sir Charles, 29–0028—29–0243
Elliott, John F., 70–0200—70–0418
Ellis, Elise Brooks, 32–0008—32–0071
Ellis, Richard, 29–0028—29–0242
Ellis, Towson, 32–0008
Ellis, W. A., & Company, 22–0247
Ellis County, Texas, 77–0004
Ellis County Land & Cattle Company, 77–0004
Ellison, Benjamin, 29–0028—29–0243
Ellison, Joe F., 77–0004
El Paso, Texas, 70–0200—70–0418
Elwood, Ella, 78–0019
Emory, R. M., 56–0005
Empresarios, 23–0002—23–4503
England, John S., 23–0002—23–4503
English, James, 72–0524—72–1992
Ennis, Cornelius, 23–0002—23–4503; 72–0524—72–1992
Ennis, Texas, 74–0019
Episcopal church, 23–0002—23–4503; 40–0027; 52–0122; 75–0005; 79–0001
Erath, George B., 29–0028—29–0243
Erath County, Texas, 78–0014
Erhard, Fred W., 30–0895
Erhard, Peter H., 14–0030; 77–0004
Erlangen, Germany, 36–1202
Ernst, E. B., 79–0011
Estiva, Jose Ignacio, 23–0002—23–4503
Eubank, T. A., 77–0004
Eufaula, Alabama, 22–0247
Evans, Charles J., 72–0524—72–1992
Evans, Elizabeth, 73–0055—73–0341
Eve, Joseph, 29–0028—29–0243
Everett, Edward, 28–0005—28–0036; 28–0293; 79–0021
Everitt, Stephen Hendrickson, 23–0002—23–4503; 73–0055—73–0341

Ewing, P. K., 75–0004
Ezell, John, 23–0002—23–4503

Fairbanks, Alfred G., 19–0027
Fairfield, Texas, 23–0002—23–4503; 24–0007—24–0035
Fairview, Texas, 22–0023; 28–0293
Fall, Philip H., 35–0018—35–0122
Falligant, Andress, 62–0003—62–0200
Falls County, Texas, 22–0247; 79–0014
Fannin, James Walker, 23–0002—23–4503; 29–0028—29–0243; 72–0001
Fant, Arthur A., Sr., 71–0196
Farenotld, Frances, 78–0023
Farinholt, A. S., 22–0153—22–0246
Farish, Oscar, 23–0002—23–4503; 51–0004—51–0125; 70–0425—70–0474
Farmers' Loan & Trust Company, 28–0233
Farmville, Virginia, 22–0057—22–0152
Fassbender family, 79–0016
Fatio, Felipe, papers, 36–0002
Faubus, Orval E., 71–0387
Faye, Stanley, 62–0003—62–0200
Fayette County, Texas, 23–0002—23–4503; 27–0044—27–0699; 42–0004—
    42–0231; 78–0014
Fayetteville, Arkansas, 42–0004—42–0231
Fenn, John R., 29–0028—29–0243
Ferguson, J. J., 25–0525—25–0552
Ferguson, Miriam Amanda, 28–0295
Ferries, 69–0276
Field, Cyrus, 79–0021
Fields, Richard, 23–0002—23–4503; 29–0028—29–0243
Fields, William A., 23–0002—23–4503; 70–0200—70–0418
Filer, Frederick, 22–0247
Fillmore, Millard, 79–0021
Film making, 77–0014
Finlay, George P., 79–0021
Finnie, J. R., 74–0019
Finsel, E., 79–0011
Fire Department notebook, 30–0839
First Baptist Church of Galveston, papers, 79–0000. *See also* Baptist church
First Hutchings-Sealy National Bank, 79–0005; ledgers, 80–0001
First National Bank of Galveston, 40–0027; records, 72–1994; 80–0001
First Presbyterian Church of Galveston, letters, 70–0163—70–0170; 72–
    1995; papers, 76–0039; 78–0014. *See also* Presbyterian church
First Texas Cavalry Company roll, 77–0011
Fischer, George, 29–0028—29–0243
Fisher, Frederick K., 40–0027
Fisher, George, 23–0002—23–4503; 36–0003—36–0009
Fisher, James J., 73–0055—73–0341
Fisher, Lewis, 76–0019

118

Fisher, Samuel Rhoads, 23–0002—23–4503; 29–0028—29–0243; 72–0001; 74–0019
Fisher, Samuel W., 72–0524—72–1992
Fisher, Walter O., 74–0019
Fisher, William S., 29–0028—29–0243
Fisher County, Texas, 78–0014
Fiske, George A., 77–0003
Flake, Ferdinand, 23–0002—23–4503; 29–0028—29–0243
Flake's Evening Bulletin, 29–0028—29–0243
Flanders, Charles N., 22–0023
Flatonia, Texas, 70–0200—70–0418; 79–0011; 79–0020
Flatonia Men's Choir, 79–0011
Fleming, J. R., 74–0019
Fletcher & Blunt, 79–0013
Flight (ship), 23–0002—23–4503; 72–0001
Flores, Gaspar, 23–0002—23–4503
Fly, W. S., 35–0018—35–0122
Focke, Georgiana Dorothea Marckmann, 04–0028
Focke, John, papers, 04–0028
Follett, A. G., Jr., 28–0061—28–0101
Fontaine, S. F., 78–0014
Fontaine, Sherman A., correspondence, 71–0192—71–0195
Food processing, 74–0018
Foote, Henry Stuart, 29–0028—29–0243
Footman, John, 23–4902—23–4908
Forbes, John, 29–0028—29–0243
Ford, Elizabeth, 73–0055—73–0341
Ford, H. C., 74–0019
Ford, John S., 29–0028—29–0243
Ford, William, 73–0055—73–0341
Forney, Texas, 22–0023
Forrest, Moreau, 72–0001
Forrester, John, 29–0028—29–0243
Fort Bend County, Texas, 23–0002—23–4503; 56–0005; 73–0055—73–0341; 78–0014
Fort Crockett, Galveston, 77–0030
Fort Point, 73–0381
Fort Point Light Station journal, 73–0381
Fort Tremont, South Carolina, 77–0030
Fort Worth, Texas, 22–0247; 70–0200—70–0418; 74–0019
Fortune, Jan Isbelle, 77–0005
Fowler, Andrew J., 29–0028—29–0243
Fowler, Bradford C., 29–0028—29–0243
Fowler, Charles, 27–0044—27–0699; 28–0061—28–0101; 70–0200—70–0418; 79–0005
Fowler, Charles, Jr., 79–0005
Fowler, John H., 29–0028—29–00243
Fowler, Linda, 19–0027
Fowler, Littlejon, 29–0028—29–0243

Fowler, M. W., 29–0028—29–0243
Fox, Warren F., papers, 79–0009
Frankfort, Kentucky, 04–0001—04–0007
Franklin, Benjamin C., 23–0002—23–4503; 29–0028—29–0243
Franklin, Robert Morris, papers, 28–0061—28–0101
Frantz, Joe B., 79–0005
Frederich, J., 23–0002—23–4503; 28–0156—28–0170
Frederick, W. J., 77–0004
Fredericksburg, Virginia, 22–0023
Freedmen's Bureau. *See* United States Bureau of Refugees, Freedmen, and Abandoned Lands
Freemasonry, 28–0293; 77–0003; 79–0015
Freeport, Texas, 79–0015
Freestone County, Texas, 72–0524—72–1992
Freiberg, Klein & Company, 78–0014
French, in Texas, 25–0591; 47–0001; 47–0002; 69–0274
French Benevolent Society of Galveston, 25–0591
Frenkel, A., & Son, 78–0014
Fresenius, J. P., 32–0008
Fritz, Bertha, 79–0020
Fromm, W., 79–0011
Frost, Meigs O., 77–0005
Frost, S. M., Jr., 77–0004
Fry, Ray, 79–0020
Fulbright, J. W., 71–0386
Fuller, Alice Campbell, 79–0005; 79–0029
Fuller, Aubrey Vance, 76–0019; 79–0029
Fuller, George F., 35–0018—35–0122
Fulmore, Z. T., 35–0018—35–0122
Fulton, Roger Lawson, 70–0200—70–0418; 79–0008
Furley, C. A., 22–0247
Fur trade, 04–0021

Gabia, Alexis de, 69–0274
Gahagan, M. J., 76–0019
Gahagan, Margaret, 79–0020
Gahan, Eliza, 22–0247
Gahan, William J., 22–0247
Gaines, James, 23–0002—23–4503; 29–0028—29–0243
Gainesville, Texas, 74–0019
Galbraith, Bessie Campbell, 79–0029
Galveston (novel), 76–0022
Galveston:
—Battle of, 42–0004—42–0231; 77–0002
—beautification, 37–0003
—calendar, 36–1203
—City Council, 69–0275; 71–0385; 78–0023; 79–0006
—city engineer, 68–0143—68–0147
—City of, 76–0023; papers, 79–0008

—commerce, 33–0041—33–0093; 33–0097; 34–0003—34–0018; 42–0004—42–0231; 67–0080; 69–0274; 70–0100—70–0162; 70–1287; 72–0111—72–0308; 72–0524—72–1992; 73–0055—73–0341; 74–0008; 75–0010; 76–0031; 77–0005; 78–0025; 78–0027; 79–0004; 79–0026
—commission government, 76–0042
—description, 27–0041; 50–0001; 68–0158; 76–0038
—education, 76–0032; 77–0036; 78–0028; 79–0015. *See also* Galveston Independent School District
—fires and fire fighting, 23–0002—23–4503; 30–0839; 32–0041
—fortifications, 30–0849
—founding of, 76–0024
—historical writings, 29–0028—29–0243; 51–0004—51–0125; 79–0017; 62–0003—62–0200; 50–0307
—Island, west end, 50–0307
—mayor, 68–0143—68–0147
—militia, 70–0425—70–0474
—planning, 77–0036
—politics, 69–0275; 79–0008
—Port of, 22–0247; 23–0002—23–4503; 25–0001—25–0521; 27–0701; 30–0200; 36–1205—36–1207; 55–0004; 70–0200—70–0418; 75–0002; 76–0023; 79–0012; 79–0022; 79–0037. *See also* Galveston Wharf Company
—reminiscences, 68–0158
—seawall, 28–0061—28–0101; 34–0021—34–0030; 76–0019
—Sister City program, 79–0028
—social life, 30–0895; 76–0017; 77–0029
—utilities, 77–0019
—water supply, 79–0008
Galveston, Houston & Henderson Railroad Company, 33–0097; 78–0014
Galveston & Brazos Navigation Company, 33–0014—33–0020; 46–0002
Galveston & Eastern Texas Railway Company, 24–0007—24–0035
Galveston & Houston Packet Line, 23–0002—23–4503
Galveston & Rio Grande Railway Company, 78–0014
Galveston & Western Railway Company, 22–0247; affidavit, 30–0950; 78–0014; 79–0005; records, 79–0032
Galveston Artillery Company, 30–0896; 75–0004; 77–0022
Galveston Art League, records, 52–0123
Galveston Bagging & Cordage Company, 72–1995
Galveston Bank & Trust Company, 33–0097; 78–0009; 78–0025; 80–0001
Galveston Brewing Company, 79–0013
Galveston Chamber of Commerce, 32–0005; 36–0010; 77–0005; 78–0014
Galveston City Chapter, 69–0276; 78–0028; 79–0006
Galveston City Company, 22–0247; 23–0002—23–4503; 25–0001—25–0521; 46–0002; 51–0004—51–0125; 52–0122; 69–0266—69–0273; 73–0055—73–0341
Galveston City party, records, 79–0022
Galveston City Railway Company, 78–0014; 79–0008
Galveston city sexton reports, 52–0030—52–0121; 79–0036
Galveston Civilian & Gazette, 23–0002—23–4504; 29–0028—29–0243

Galveston Public Library, 51–0004—51–0125
Galveston public schools, 76–0032; 78–0014
Galveston Quartette Society, records, 78–0011
Galveston Rifles Company, papers, 28–0102—28–0126
Galveston Rope & Twine Company, 78–0014
Galveston Seamen's Home, 36–1205—36–1207
Galveston Sewer Company, 78–0014
Galveston Southern Cotton Press & Manufacturing Company, 23–0002—
    23–4503; 78–0014
Galveston Suburban Improvement Company, 78–0014
Galveston–Texas City pilots, logbooks, 75–0002
Galveston University, 71–0385
Galveston Water Works, 79–0008
Galveston West End Company, 78–0017
Galveston Wharf & Cotton Press Company, 48–0050
Galveston Wharf Company, 23–0002—23–4503; 27–0044—27–0699; 27–
    0702; 77–0003; 78–0012; 78–0014; 79–0012
Galvez, Bernardo de, 29–0028—29–0243; land grant, 31–1163
Gamage family, 78–0014
Gano, Franklin M., 22–0247
Gano Brothers, 77–0004
Gardening, 79–0007
Gardner, Mary, 79–0020
Garfield, James, 24–0088
Garner, John C., 72–1995
Garner, John Nance, 71–0387
Garrett, A. H. P., 73–0055—73–0341
Garrett, Christopher C., 78–0014
Garrison, George Pierce, 35–0018—35–0122
Garten Verein, records, 30–0895; 72–1995
Gatesville, Texas, 74–0019
Gautier, Pierre, 69–0274; 70–1179—70–1189
Gautier family, papers, 69–0274
Geeslin, R. C., 62–0003—62–0200
Genealogy, 75–0005; 77–0047; 79–0010
General Rusk (vessel), 25–0525—25–0552
Gengler, Matt, 79–0013
Gengler, Peter, & Company, papers, 76–0031
George, James A., 70–0200—70–0418
George, R. F., 24–0007—24–0035
Georgetown, Kentucky, 70–0475—70–0492
Georgetown, Texas, 23–0002—23–4503; 35–0018—35–0122; 78–0023
German Evangelical Lutheran Church, 46–0002
Germans, in Galveston, 04–0028; 30–0028—30–0196; 30–0895; 36–1202;
    46–0002; 56–0005; 76–0003; 77–0004; 79–0011
Germans, in Texas, 79–0011
Germand, John H., 29–0028—29–0243
Gernand, J. H., 76–0019
Gettysburg, Battle of, 74–0010

Gibson's Battery, 55–0001
Gidding, Texas, 30–0197
Giddings, DeWitt Clinton, 22–0153—22–0246; 70–0200—70–0418
Giddings, Jabez Deming, 22–0153—22–0246; 23–0002—23–4503; 70–1150—70–1178; 72–0524—72–1992
Gifford, G. C., 79–0014
Gifford & Torgason, 79–0014
Gildersleeve, Phillip, 22–0153—22–0246
Gillaspie, James, 23–0002—23–4503; 29–0028—29–0243
Gillespie, C. B., 29–0028—29–0243
Gillespie, Robert Addison, 29–0028—29–0243
Gillespie County, Texas, 78–0014
Girard, Stephen, 79–0005
Girardeau, Gertrude, 19–0027
Giraud, F., 72–1995
Girls' Literary Club of Galveston, records, 67–0021—67–0022
Glasscock, George M., 29–0028—29–0243
Glenblythe plantation, 33–0004—33–0012
Glidden, C. J., 78–0014
Goals for Galveston, records, 77–0036
Goddard, William H., 23–0002—23–4503; receipts, 30–0892; 70–1150—70–1178
Goggan, Thomas, 78–0014
Goldthwaite, Joseph G., 28–0061—28–0101
Goldthwaite, Texas, 79–0005
Goliad, Texas, 23–0002—23–4503; 73–0055—73–0341
Gomez, Juana, 46–0002
Gonzales, Mrs. Boyer, 52–0123
Gonzales, Manuel, 79–0021
Gonzales, Texas, 23–0002—23–4503; 35–0018—35–0122; 70–0200—70–0418
Gonzales family, 78–0009
Gonzales County, Texas, 22–0247; 23–0002—23–4503
Gooch, John Young, 75–0004
Goode, John D., 72–0524—72–1992
Goodwin, G. I., 74–0019
Goodwin, John W., 74–0019
Goodwyn, Alice, 22–0023
Gordon, Sidney, 28–0293
Goree, Thomas Jewett, 77–0004
Garibaldi, G., 79–0021
Gosse, Auguste, 70–1179—70–1189
Gottingen, Germany, 22–0023
Gould, William L., 74–0019
Govan, Scotland, 76–0016
Grabau, Theodor, 51–0004—51–0125
Grace Episcopal Church, 33–0097
Grade raising, 22–0024; 32–0066
Graff, J., 23–0002—23–4503

Grahame, William, 24–0088
Granbury, Hiram Bronson, 29–0028—29–0243
Grand Lodge of Texas Freemasonry. *See* Freemasonry
Grand Opera House, 76–0016; programs, 76–0017
Grant, Ben, 78–0023
Grant, James, 23–0002—23–4503; 29–0028—29–0243
Grant, James C., 70–0425—70–0474
Grant, Ulysses Simpson, letter, 04–0044; 24–0088; 79–0021
Grass, John R., 78–0014
Graves, Jerome B., 30–0850—30–0890
Graves, Richard, 30–0850—30–0890
Gray, Alfred G., 72–0001
Gray, Allen Charles, 29–0028—29–0243
Gray, Franklin C., 29–0028—29–0243
Gray, James Newcomer, 23–0002—23–4503
Gray, Mabry B., 29–0028—29–0243
Gray, Millie, diary, 50–0437
Gray, Peter W., 23–0002—23–4503; 29–0028—29–0243; 69–0266; 72–0524—72–1992
Gray, William Fairfax, 23–0002—23–4503; 29–0028—29–0243; 51–0004—51–0125
Grayson, Peter W., 23–0002—23–4503; 25–0001—25–0521; 29–0028—29–0243; 74–0018
Grayson, Thomas Wigg, 70–1200—70–1258
Grayson County, Texas, 78–0014
Great Southern Sulphur Company, 78–0019
Greeley, Horace, 79–0021
Green, Duff, 29–0028—29–0243; 46–0002
Green, Laura J., 78–0009
Green, Thomas, 23–0002—23–4503; 46–0002; 51–0004—51–0125
Green, Thomas Jefferson, 23–0002—23–4503; 29–0028—29–0243; 51–0004—51–0125
Greenleve, Block & Company, records, 33–0041—33–0093; 72–1995
Greenlow, John O., 51–0004—51–0125
Greenville, New York, 36–0045—36–1201
Greenway, E. M., Jr., 78–0014
Greer, John S., 28–0102—28–0128
Greeting cards, 76–0027
Gregory, Elliott W., 23–0002—23–4503
Gregory, Ephraim, 22–0023
Gregory, Thomas C., & Son, 79–0014
Gresham, Walter, papers, 22–0247; 28–0233; 30–0950; 78–0014; 79–0008; 79–0019
Gresham, Walter, Jr., 79–0011
Gresham, Jones & Spencer, 22–0247
Gresham & Jones, 22–0247
Gresham & Mann, 22–0247
Grey, William Fairfax, 46–0002
Griffin, John, 52–0030—52–0121

Griffing, Willis, 22–0023
Grimes, Jesse, 29–0028—29–0243
Grimes, W. H., 23–0002—23–4503
Grimes County, Texas, 23–0002—23–4503; 78–0014
Groce, Leonard Waller, 23–0002—23–4503
Groce, T. J., 78–0014
Grocers, 76–0031
Groesbeck, John D., 23–0002—23–4503; 46–0002; 51–0004—51–0125
Grooms, Alfred, 77–0004
Grosse Tête Flying Artillery, report, 44–0007
Grover, Charles H., 51–0004—51–0125
Grover, Eliza A., 51–0004—51–0125
Grover, George W., 23–0002—23–4503; 51–0004—51–0125; 72–1995
Grover, Walter E., article, 68–0158
Gruner, Siegfried, 56–0005
Grunewald, Mrs. L. P., 36–0045—36–1201
Guadalupe County, Texas, 23–0002—23–4503; 78–0014
Guaranty Building & Loan Company, 78–0019
Guenther, Hans, 56–0005
Guerrero, Vicente Ramon, 23–0002—23–4503
Gugett, Phyllis, 79–0020
Gulf, Colorado & Santa Fe Railway Company, 22–0247; records, 28–0233;
    authorization, 32–0001; 32–0008; 78–0014
Gulf, Western Texas & Pacific Railway Company, 56–0005
Gulf Interstate Railway Company, 78–0014
Gulf Intracoastal Canal, papers, 71–0386
Gulf City Street Railway & Real Estate Company, 73–0004—73–0007
Gullett Gin Company, 79–0013
Gumpert, Kate, 78–0009; 78–0014
Gurney, Mrs. Harold B., 62–0003—62–0200
Gutierrez de Lara, Jose Bernardo Maximiliano, 23–0002—23–4503; 29–
    0028—29–0243

Hacienda de Mirador, Mexico, 22–0247
Haitt, James S., 74–0019
Hale, Edward Everett, 35–0018—35–0122
Hale, William G., 23–0002—23–4503; 73–0055—73–0341
Halifax, Nova Scotia, 42–0232—42–0287
Hall, Edward, 25–0001—25–0521
Hall, Julietta, 73–0055—73–0341
Hall, Nicholas C., 23–0002—23–4503
Hall, W. W., 29–0028—29–0243
Hall, Warren D. C., 23–0002—23–4503; 29–0028—29–0243; 73–0055—
    73–0341
Hamilton, Andrew Jackson, 73–0055—73–0341
Hamilton, Elizabeth M., 51–0004—51–0125
Hamilton, James, 23–0002—23–4503; 29–0028—29–0243; 51–0004—51–
    0125
Hamilton, Morgan C., 29–0028—29–0243

Hammand, G. H., 72–0524—72–1992
Hammeken, George Lewis, 70–1179—70–1189
Hancock, John, 70–0200—70–0418
Hand, E. D., 70–0100—70–0162
Hands Mill, Texas, 70–0100—70–0162
Hann, J. N., 51–0004—51–0125
Hanna, J. J., 73–0055—73–0341
Hanna & Fahey, real estate records, 77–0007
Hannay, R. E., 74–0019
Hannay, R. M., 23–0002—23–4503; 73–0055—73–0341
Hansford, John M., 29–0028—29–0243
Hardaway, Samuel G., 29–0028—29–0243
Harde & Company, 22–0247
Hardee, W. O., 25–0553—25–0567
Hardeman, Bailey, 29–0028—29–0243
Hardeman, Sam, 22–0153—22–0246
Hardeman, Thomas M., 29–0028—29–0243
Hardeman, William P., 29–0028—29–0243
Hardin, Augustin Blackburn, 29–0028—29–0243
Hardin, Benjamin Watson, 29–0028—29–0243
Hardin, Franklin, 29–0028—29–0243
Hardin, Dr. Martin, 19–0027
Hardin, William, 23–0002—23–4503; 29–0028—29–0243
Hardware, 74–0008
Hardy, H. C., 72–0524—72–1992
Harlock, Mrs. John, 22–0247
Harn, A. D., 23–4971—23–4993
Harn, W. F. D., 23–4971—23–4993
Harriet Lane (ship), 28–0005—28–0036; 77–0002
Harrington, H. H., 24–0068—24–0070
Harrington, John A., 72–0524—72–1992
Harris (vessel), 23–0002—23–4503
Harris, A. J., 74–0019
Harris, Annie Pleasants, memoirs, 65–0009
Harris, Bayliss E., 79–0022
Harris, Brantly, papers, 76–0023
Harris, David, 23–0002—23–4503; 29–0028—29–0243
Harris, E. F., 78–0014
Harris, E. S., 72–0524—72–1992
Harris, Ed J., papers, 78–0023
Harris, Francis Kay, 78–0028
Harris, J. C., 78–0014
Harris, John Richardson, 23–0002—23–4503; 29–0028—29–0243
Harris, John W., 65–0009; 73–0004—73–0007
Harris, John Woods, 23–0002—23–4503; 25–0522; 25–0553—25–0567;
    papers, 74–0019
Harris, Pryor Nance, journal, 63–0002
Harris, William Plunkett, 23–0002—23–4503; 72–0001
Harris & Monk, 77–0004

Harrisburg, Texas, 23–0002—23–4503; 25–0525—25–0552; 28–0293; 73–0055—73–0341; 74–0018; 79–0011

Harris County, 22–0023; 23–0002—23–4503; 24–0007—24–0035; 25–0525—25–0552; 28–0293; 30–0197; 42–0004—42–0231; 56–0005; 62–0003—62–0200; 69–0266—69–0273; 72–0001; 72–0524—72–1992; 72–1995; 73–0055—73–0341; 74–0018; 75–0004; 78–0014; 78–0017; 79–0015

Harrison, Benjamin, 73–0055—73–0341

Harrison, Isham, 70–0475—70–0492

Harrison, Jonas, 29–0028—29–0243

Harrison County, 22–0247

Harrodsburg, Kentucky, 25–0553—25–0567

Hart, Edmund J., 22–0153—22–0246; 72–0524—72–1992

Hart, James K., 22–0247

Hart, S., 24–0007—24–0035

Hartel, Fred, 76–0019

Hartford, Connecticut, 22–0247

Hart Land & Import Company, 77–0004

Hartley, Oliver Cromwell, 29–0028—29–0243

Hartman, A., 22–0247

Hartmann, J. C., 79–0011

Haskell, Charles R., 29–0028—29–0243

Haskell County, Texas, 78–0017

Hassmann family, 79–0016

Hatch, Lucien B., 22–0247

Haupt, Lewis M., 70–0200—70–0418

Hawkins, Charles Edward, 29–0028—29–0243; 72–0001

Hawkins, Eugene A., Jr., 46–0002

Hawley, Robert Bradley, 78–0009

Hawthorne, Mrs. Paul, 62–0003—62–0200

Hayes, Arthur E., 78–0017

Hayes, Rutherford B., 24–0088

Hayes, Webb C., 24–0088

Hays, John Coffee, 29–0028—29–0243; 70–1200—70–1258

Heard, William Jones Elliot, 29–0028—29–0243

Hearne, H. R., 72–0524—72–1992

Hearne, Mrs. R. W., 35–0018—35–0122

Hearst, George, 79–0021

Hebrew Cemetery No. 1 of Galveston, 71–0207

Heffron, Isaac, 77–0004

Heidenheimer, Sampson, 22–0247

Heidenheimer Castle, 72–1995

Heinrich, Mrs. Paul, 79–0020

Heitman, F. W., 77–0004

Helena Public Library, Montana, 78–0019

Hellmers, Mrs. L., 77–0004

Hemingway, Matt, 62–0003—62–0200

Hemphill, John, 29–0028—29–0243

Hempstead, Texas, 23–0002—23–4503; 70–0100—70–0162; 71–0326—71–0370; 73–0055—73–0341; 79–0011
Hemsworth, Thomas, 23–0002—23–4503; 51–0004—51–0125
Henck, C. J., 76–0016
Henck, Jacob, 46–0002; 78–0009
Henderson, James W., 23–0002—23–4503; 29–0028—29–0243
Henderson, Texas, 70–0200—70–0418
Henderson & Ardrey, 79–0027
Henderson County, Texas, 78–0014
Hendley, Joseph J., 22–0153—22–0246; 23–0002—23–4503; letters, 75–0001—75–0001a
Hendley, William, & Company, records, 22–0153—22–0246; 23–0002—23–4503
Hendley Building, 27–0701; 71–0192—71–0195; 72–1995
Hendricks, George B., 77–0004
Hendricks, Harry, 72–0524—72–1992
Henlock, William, 76–0016
Henry, Ellen, 79–0019
Herd, R. H., 49–0001—49–0006
Herndon, John Hunter, 23–4971—23–4993
Herrera, Simon, 29–0028—29–0242
Herring, William P., 70–0100—70–0162; 73–0055—73–0341
Hersey, Mrs. O. V., 62–0003—62–0200
Hertz, L. W., 29–0028—29–0243
Hess, Anton, 46–0002
Hessly, John, 33–0097
Heston, H. G., 22–0247
Heydon, Julius, 79–0011
Hicks, J. F., 73–0055—73–0341
Highland Bayou, 74–0010
Highland Park, Texas, 78–0022
Highsmith, Sam, 29–0028—29–0243
Hill, Asa C., 29–0028—29–0243
Hill, Benjamin F., 70–1200—70–1258
Hill, George Washington, 23–0002—23–4503; 29–0028—29–0243; 72–0001
Hill, J. M., 35–0018—35–0122
Hill, John Christopher Columbus, 29–0028—29–0243
Hill, William Pinckney, 70–1150—70–1178
Hill County, 78–0014
Hillsboro, Texas, 35–0018—35–0122; 74–0019
Hinton, A. C., 72–0001
Hirzel, Richard, papers, 30–0998
Historic American Buildings Survey, Galveston survey records, 72–1995
Historic preservation, 72–1995; 74–0011; 79–0037
Hitchcock, Frank, 70–0425—70–0474
Hitchcock, Lent Munson, 23–0002—23–4503; 73–0055—73–0341
Hitchcock, Texas, 76–0016
Hitchcock & Company, 23–0002—23–4503; papers, 44–0002—44–0005

Hobby, Alfred Marmaduke, letter, 32–0005
Hobby, B. M., 75–0004
Hockley, George Washington, 23–0002—23–4503; 29–0028—29–0243; 72–0001
Hodges, E. G., 22–0247
Hodson, Alice Minot, 76–0016
Hodson, George, 76–0016
Hodson, James Densmore, 76–0016
Hodson, Rebecca Bell, letter, 70–0035; 76–0016
Hodson, Robert B., 76–0016
Hoffman, Adolph Gustav Carl, 14–0030
Hogg, Alex, 70–0200—70–0418
Holcombe, John C., 36–0045—36–1201
Holland, Bird, 28–0102—28–0128
Holland, Clarence S., 71–0386
Holland, Gustavus, 72–0524—72–1992
Hollandale, Texas, 72–0524—72–1992
Holliday, L., 74–0019
Holliday, Thomas, 22–0247
Holman, William R., 79–0020
Holmes, Oliver Wendell, 28–0295; 79–0021
Holt, Charles A., Jr., papers, 24–0148—24–0151
Holt, John S., 76–0019
Holt, O. T., 75–0004
Holtzclaw, Mary A., 22–0247
Hood, John Bell, 25–0553—25–0567; 29–0028—29–0243
Hood County, Texas, 78–0014
Hood's Texas Brigade, 74–0010
Hopkins, A. R., 79–0019
Hopkins, H. L., 22–0024
Hopkins, John W., 36–0045—36–1201
Hopkins, Matthew, 70–1179—70–1189
Hornsby, J. L., 22–0153—22–0246
Horsley, Charles A., 77–0004
Horton, Alexander, 29–0028—29–0243
Hoston, A. J., 35–0018—35–0122
Hotels, 30–0956—30–0991
Houston, F. W., 35–0018—35–0122
Houston, Sam, 23–0002—23–4503; 25–0522; 28–0295; 31–0001—31–1096; 31–1231—31–1243; 35–0018—35–0122; 49–0001—49–0006; 51–0004—51–0125; bank draft, 62–0001; 72–0001; 74–0018; 76–0024; 77–0012; 79–0021
Houston, Temple, 79–0021
Houston, Texas, 23–0002—23–4503; 32–0008; 35–0018—35–0122; 36–0045—36–1201; 70–0100—70–0162; 79–0015; 79–0019
Houston Weekly Commercial Review, 29–0028—29–0243
Howard, Elizabeth, 23–0002—23–4503; 73–0055—73–0341
Howard, George Thomas, 29–0028—29–0243
Howard, Thomas B., 28–0102—28–0128

Howard, Thomas S., 29–0028—29–0243
Howard, Thomas Wade, 27–0044—27–0699
Howard, Volney Erskine, 23–0002—23–4503; 29–0028—29–0243
Howard Association of Galveston, records, 14–0030; 23–0002—23–4503
Howeth, W. W., 74–0019
Hoyle, A. T., 77–0004
Hoyt, Lieutenant ———, 72–0001
Hubbell, Henry, 23–0002—23–4503; papers, 70–0100—70–0162; 73–
    0055—73–0341
Huckting, D., 79–0011
Hudson, Joe, 78–0017
Hudson, William M., 22–0247
Huff, Donaldson, 27–0044—27–0699
Huff, John, 23–0002—23–4503; 30–0850—30–0890
Huffaker, Melvin, 77–0004
Huffmaster, James Taylor, 04–0001—04–0007
Huffmaster, Joseph, 04–0001—04–0007
Hughes, Charles H., 77–0004
Hughes, Edward Smallwood, 77–0004
Hughes, William Edgar, 70–0200—70–0418
Hull, Wager, 78–0017
Humble Oil & Refinery Company, 78–0017
Hume, F. Charles, 79–0019
Hume, George T., 74–0019
Hume, J. L., 74–0019
Humphreys, Geraldine Davis, 77–0013
Humphreys, Robert Wade, 77–0013
Humphries, Jesse, 73–0055—73–0341
Hunt, Davis, 36–0045—36–1201
Hunt, Memucan, 23–0002—23–4503; 29–0028—29–0243; papers, 70–
    0510—70–1138; 72–0001; 74–0018
Hunter, John Dunn, 23–0002—23–4503; 29–0028—29–0243
Hunter, Johnson, 23–0002—23–4503
Hunter, John Warren, 29–0028—29–0243
Hunter, William L., 23–0002—23–4503; 29–0028—29–0243
Huntington, Collis Potter, 28–0295; 44–0016; 46–0002; 70–0200—70–0418
Huntsville, Texas, 23–0002—23–4503; 72–0524—72–1992
Hurd, Ann Gardner, 75–0005
Hurd, Ella Elizabeth, 75–0005
Hurd, James Gardner, 23–0002—23–4503; 29–0028—29–0243; 75–0005
Hurd, Norman, 23–0002—23–4503; 29–0028—29–0243; 72–0001; 75–0005
Hurd-Gardner family history, 75–0005
Hurlbut, Samuel B., 77–0003
Hurley, C. W., & Company, 77–0004
Hurricane of 1900, 04–0028; 24–0148—24–0151; 25–0586; 46–0006; 49–
    0014—49–0021; 51–0004—51–0125; 68–0039; 68–0057—68–0074;
    68–0143—68–0147; 76–0016; 76–0026
Hurricane of 1915, 15–0001; 48–0103; 71–0192—71–0195
Hurricane of 1961 (Carla), 62–0201; 65–0002; 71–0162; 71–0196

Hussar Cavalry, 31–1178
Huston, Felix, 29–0028—29–0242
Hutchings, Elise, 32–0008—32–0071
Hutchings, J. H., 46–0002
Hutchings, John C., 70–0200—70–0418
Hutchings, John H., 49–0001—49–0006
Hutchings, Sealy & Company, 23–0002—23–4503; papers, 52–0019—52–0023; 78–0014; 80–0001
Hutchings family, 78–0017
Hutchings Joint Stock Association, 78–0017; 80–0001
Hutchings-Sealy National Bank, 49–0001—49–0006; 78–0017
Hutchison, Anderson, 29–0028—29–0243
Hutchinson, Jennie T., 24–0088
Hyatt, John, 79–0005

Iams, Basil G., 29–0028—29–0243
Iams, John, 29–0028—29–0243
Ibbotson, Joseph S., 62–0003—62–0200; 79–0020
Iglehart, R. H., 62–0003—62–0200
Iglehart & Leonard, 22–0247
Illies, John H., papers, 23–0002—23–4503; 36–1202
Illies-McKenzie family papers, 36–1202
Immigration, 23–0002—23–4503; 33–0004—33–0012
Independence, Texas, 23–0002—23–4503; 23–4920—23–4932
Independence (ship), 72–0001
Indianola, Texas, 23–0002—23–4503; 70–0100—70–0162
Indianola Bulletin, 29–0028—29–0243
Indians. *See* Native Americans
Ing, Dr.———, 23–0002—23–4503
Ingalls, H. A., 78–0014
Ingersoll, R. G., 79–0021
Ingram, Elijah, 29–0028—29–0243
Ingram, Ira, 23–0002—23–4503; 29–0028—29–0243
Ingram, John, 29–0028—29–0243
Ingram, Seth, 23–0002—23–4503; 29–0028—29–0243; 30–0850—30–0890
Insurance, 23–0002—23–4503; 80–0003
International Creosote & Construction Company, 30–0896
International Shipbuilding Company, 69–0276
Investments, 77–0029
Invincible (ship), 23–0002—23–4503; 72–0001
Ireland, John, 70–0200—70–0418
Irion, Robert Anderson, 23–0002—23–4503; 29–0028—29–0243
Irrigation, 23–0002—23–4503
Irvine, Marcellus, 77–0004
Irvine, Robert C., 77–0004
Irving, Washington, 28–0295
Isbell, William, 29–0028—29–0243
Island City Abstract & Loan Company, 78–0014
Ives, Charles, 25–0001—25–0521

Jack, Laura Harrison, 23–0002—23–4503; 70–0475—70–0492
Jack, Patrick Churchill, 23–0002—23–4503; 29–0028—29–0243
Jack, Spencer H., 23–0002—23–4503; 29–0028—29–0243
Jack, Thomas McKinney, 23–0002—23–4503; 23–5212; 70–0475—70–0492
Jack, William Houston, 23–0002—23–4503; 29–0028—29–0243; 70–0475—70–0492
Jack family, papers, 70–0475—70–0492
Jackson, Abner, 70–0100—70–0162
Jackson, Andrew, 23–0002—23–4503; 28–0295; letter, 77–0012; 79–0021; 80–0010
Jackson, Mrs. J. E., 79–0020
Jackson County, Texas, 23–4902—23–4908; 79–0014
Jacques, William Budd, papers, 70–1200—70–1258
James, W. A., 79–0020
Jasper County, Texas, 31–1180—31–1183
Jefferson, Thomas, 79–0021
Jefferson Barracks, Missouri, 32–0008
Jefferson County, Mississippi, 36–0045—36–1201
Jefferson County, Texas, 23–0002—23–4503; 51–0004—51–0125; 78–0014
Jenkins, Henry, 23–0002—23–4503
Jennings, Robert T., 22–0247
Jersig, Wenzel, 79–0011
Jersig family, 79–0009
Jewish Immigrants Information Bureau, 79–0033
Jewry, in Galveston, 71–0207; 79–0033
Jockusch, John W., 74–0015
Jockusch, Julius, 62–0003—62–0200
Jockusch, Frederick, & Company, 23–0002—23–4503
Jockusch, J. W., & Company, 23–0002—23–4503
John, James, 78–0009
Johnson, A. Sidney, 79–0021
Johnson, C. C., 79–0027
Johnson, F. N., 70–0100—70–0162
Johnson, Francis White, 23–0002—23–4503
Johnson, Frank C., papers, 79–0015
Johnson, Frank W., 29–0028—29–0243
Johnson, H. M., 77–0004
Johnson, James R., 79–0014
Johnson, Lady Bird, 76–0027
Johnson, Lyndon Baines, 71–0387; 78–0022; 80–0002
Johnson, Marsene, 76–0019
Johnson, Middleton, 29–0028—29–0243
Johnson, P. N., 70–0100—70–0162
Johnson, Robert Dabney, 23–0002—23–4503; 70–0100—70–0162; 79–0029
Johnson, William R., 22–0247; 23–0002—23–4503; 51–0004—51–0125; 75–0004
Johnson & Gatling, 79–0027
Johnston, Albert Sidney, 23–0002—23–4503; 29–0028—29–0243; 35–0018—35–0122; letters, 70–1271—70–1272; 74–0018

Johnston, Hancock M., 35–0018—35–0122
Johnston, J. B., 72–0524—72–1992
Johnston, J. C., 30–0850—30–0890
Johnston, William, 29–0028—29–0243
J.O.L.O. Observatory, record book, 27–0701
Jones, Anson, 23–0002—23–4503; 25–0525—25–0552; 74–0018; 79–0021
Jones, Cromwell Anson, 75–0004
Jones, G. A., 23–0002—23–4503; 71–0385; 73–0055—73–0341
Jones, Henry Bradley, 28–0055—28–0060
Jones, J. B., 73–0055—73–0341
Jones, J. C., 29–0028—29–0243
Jones, James A., 70–0425—70–0474
Jones, James Henry, 70–0200—70–0418
Jones, John M., 23–0002—23–4503; 78–0014
Jones, John Rice, 23–0002—23–4503; 29–0028—29–0243
Jones, Levi, 23–0002—23–4503; 25–0001—25–0521; 29–0028—29–0243;
    46–0002; deposition, 48–0050; 49–0001—49–0006; 51–0004—51–
    0125; 52–0122; 70–0475—70–0492; 73–0055—73–0341
Jones, Lucy B., 70–0475—70–0492
Jones, Oliver, 23–0002—23–4503; 29–0028—29–0243
Jones, Randal, 23–0002—23–4503; 27–0041; 29–0028—29–0243
Jones, S. S., 22–0247
Jones, Sam W., 79–0019
Jones, Sarah F., 70–0475—70–0492
Jones, T. M., 28–0293
Jones, William Jefferson, 23–0002—23–4503; 29–0028—29–0243; 70–
    0200—70–0418; 79–0021
Jordon, C., 22–0247
Joseph, Lee, 22–0023
Joseph, N. N., 22–0023
Journey, Henry, 50–0415
Junior League of Galveston, 75–0008; 79–0005
Jursching, Karl, 79–0011

Kammerer, E. P., 78–0014
Kamsler, Henry, 74–0019
Karnes, Henry Max, 29–0028—29–0243
Kauffman, C. A., 29–0028—29–0243
Kauffman, Clara, 56–0005
Kauffman, J. Ed, 75–0004
Kauffman, Julius, 56–0005; 73–0055—73–0341
Kauffman, Mike, 74–0019
Kauffman & Runge, records and papers, 56–0005
Kauffman & Wagner, 56–0005
Kaufman, David S., 29–0028—29–0243
Kaufman, Simon, 78–0014
Kaufman County, Texas, 78–0014
Keenan, Charles A., 76–0019
Keetch, Thomas, 77–0003

Keller, Emma F., 74–0010
Keller, Ewald, 74–0010
Kelley, William D., papers, 27–0019—27–0022; 81–0003
Kelsey, Albert, 78–0019
Kelsey, H. B., 35–0018—35–0122
Kempner, Cecile, 72–0111—72–0308
Kempner, Daniel W., scrapbooks, 75–0010
Kempner, Harris, 46–0002; 78–0014
Kempner, Henrietta Blum, 52–0123
Kempner, Isaac Herbert, 65–0002; papers, 72–0111—72–0308; 76–0019;
    80–0002; 80–0003; 52–0019—52–0023
Kempner, Mary Jean, scrapbook, 72–0310; 80–0002
Kempner, Ruth Levy, papers, 69–0275; 78–0028; 80–0002
Kempner, H., Unincorporated, 80–0002—80–0003
Kempner family, 72–0111—72–0308; 79–0022; 80–0002; 80–0003
Kendall, Belle Sherman, 35–0018—35–0122; 65–0003
Kendall, George Wilkens, 29–0038—29–0243
Kennebec, Maine, 79–0019
Kennedy, E. P., 72–0001
Kennedy, W. J., 77–0004
Kennedy, William, 29–0028—29–0243
Kenney, Martin McHenry, 29–0028—29–0243
Kent, Andrew, 29–0028—29–0243
Kenyon, L. M., 22–0024
Keougl, Edward, 79–0019
Keplinger, Mrs. Leonard, 78–0017
Kerr, Hugh Peter, 23–0002—23–4503; 29–0028—29–0243
Kerr, James, 23–0002—23–4503; 29–0028—29–0243
Kerrville, Texas, 28–0293
Kershaw, Francis deSales, 74–0002
Ketchum, Edwin N., 24–0148—24–0151
Ketchum, Edwin N., residence, 65–0008
Key West, Florida, 22–0247
KGBC hurricane Carla records, 65–0002
Killer bees, 78–0024
Kilman, Ed, 62–0003—62–0200
Kimball, John P., 25–0001—25–0521
Kimble, Herbert Simms, 29–0028—29–0243
Kimble County, Texas, 78–0014
Kimley, Michael, 22–0247
King, A. C., 74–0019
King, Aaron, 29–0028—29–0243
Kinnebrew, J. L., 77–0004
Kinney, Henry Lawrence, 23–0002—23–4503; 29–0028—29–0243
Kirby, John Henry, 75–0004
Kirby, R. A., 74–0019
Kirk, John, 78–0009
Kirk, Frances, 52–0123
Kirkham, Kate, 32–0008

Kirkland, G. A., 74–0019
Kirlicks, John A., 75–0004
Kistler, Annie P., 78–0019
Klaus, R., 79–0019
Kleberg, Rudolph, 29–0028—29–0243
Kleinecke, Theodore, 22–0247
Klemm, O., 23–0002—23–4503
Klingemann, C., 79–0011
Knepper, Mrs. David W., 62–0003—62–0200
Knight, William M., 74–0019
Knoxville, Tennessee, 04–0001—04–0007
Koenig, G. E., 22–0247
Koenig, Julia, 77–0047
Kokernot, David, 23–0002—23–4503; 29–0028—29–0243
Kosse, Texas, 22–0247
Krauss, G. C., 30–0998
Kruger, Wilhelm, 28–0005—28–0036
Kuhn's Wharf, 77–0003
Kuykendall, Abner, 23–0002—23–4503; 29–0028—29–0243
Kyle, Ellen, 22–0247
Kyle, Rufus, 22–0247
Kyle, William R., 22–0247
Kyle, Texas, 70–0200—70–0418

Labaca (vessel), 23–0002—23–4503
La Baca Station, 23–0002—23–4503
Labadie, Mary Cecelia, 22–0009—22–0021
Labadie, Nicholas Descomps, papers, 22–0009—22–0021; 23–0002—23–
    4503; 70–0100—70–0162; 77–0003
Labadie, Sarah, 22–0009—22–0021
Labatt & Noble, 22–0247
Labor strikes, 76–0019
Labor union, 52–0019—52–0023
Lackland, S. M., & Company, 22–0247
Lacy, W. D., 23–0002—23–4503
Laffite, Jean, 26–0392; 27–0041; 36–0002; collection, 76–0007
Laffite brothers, 36–0002
Laffite family, records, 47–0029—47–0031
La Grange, Texas, 23–0002—23–4503; 42–0004—42–0231; 72–0524—72–
    1992; 79–0011; 79–0014
Lagrave, Anthony, 22–0009—22–0021
Laguayra, Venezuela, 73–0055—73–0341
Lake, Joseph S., 23–0002—23–4503
Lake, J. S., & Company, 23–0002—23–4503
Lake Charles, Louisiana, 71–0386
Lake Jackson, Texas, 23–0002—23–4503; 79–0015
Lallemand, Charles François Antoine, 29–0028—29–0243; 47–0001
Lamar, Lucius Quintus Cincinnatus, 79–0021

Lamar, Mirabeau Bonaparte, 23–0002—23–4503; 35–0018—35–0122; 36–0003—36–0009; 70–1200—70–1258; 79–0021

Lamb, Florence, 79–0013

Lamb, George A., 29–0028—29–0243

Lamm, Charles, 23–0002—23–4503

Lammers & Flint Cotton Factors, 78–0014

Lampasas County, Texas, 31–1165

Landers, D., 42–0004—42–0231

Landers, Henry A., 42–0004—42–0231

Land grants, 31–1163; 36–0045—36–1201; 51–0004—51–0125; 52–0122; 76–0024; 80–0010

Land use and speculation, 22–0023; 23–0002—23–4503; 24–0068—24–0070; 25–0001—25–0521; 27–0044—27–0699; 27–0702; 31–0001—31–1096; 31–1231—31–1243; 33–0004—33–0012e; 46–0002; 70–1150—70–1178; 70–1179—70–1189; 72–0524—72–1992; 74–0019; 77–0004; 77–0007; 77–0029; 78–0012; 78–0013; 78–0014; 78–0017; 79–0019; 80–0003

Lane, Walter P., 29–0028—29–0243

Lange, H. L., 76–0019

Lanham, Fritz G., 29–0028—29–0243

Lapele, Jean, 29–0028—29–0243

La Porte, Texas, 35–0018—35–0122; 74–0002

Larchmont Yacht Club, 79–0029

Laredo, Texas, 23–0002—23–4503

Laro, Arthur, 62–0003–62–0200

Lasker, Morris, 78–0021; 79–0033

Lasker Home for Children, 72–1995; records, 78–0021

Lathrop, John T. K., 72–0001

Lausen, U. J., 23–4971—23–4993

Lauterback, Louise Schott, 22–0247

Lauterback, Richard, 22–0247

La Valle, Peter J., 65–0002; 79–0020

Law, George H., Jr., 78–0014

League, Esther Yarral Wilson, 23–4909—23–4919

League, Hosea H., 23–0002—23–4503

League, John Charles, 24–0068—24–0070; 40–0027; 56–0005; papers, 77–0029; 78–0014

League, Mary D., 23–4920—23–4932; papers, 23–4997—23–5198; 56–0005

League, Nellie Ball, 24–0068—24–0070

League, Thomas Jefferson, 23–0002—23–4503; papers, 23–4920—23–4932; 23–4997—23–5198; 24–0007—24–0035; 28–0293; 73–0055—73–0341

League, Thomas Massie, 23–0002—23–4503; 23–4909—23–4919

League & Ingram, 23–0002—23–4503

League City, Texas, 24–0068—24–0070; 78–0018; 79–0015

League of Women Voters, 69–0275; records, 78–0028

Leahy, Daniel, 28–0005—28–0036

Leake, Elizabeth, 79–0020

Little Theatre of Galveston, records, 78–0026
Little Rock, Arkansas, 70–0200—70–0418
Live Oak Point, Texas, 23–0002—23–4503; 70–0425—70–0474
Liverpool, Texas, 23–0002—23–4503; 24–0068—24–0070
Livingston, Texas, 23–0002—23–4503; 71–0385
Llano County, 78–0014
Local events calendar, 36–1203
Lockett, Thomas H., 72–0524—72–1992
Lockhart, Captain Byrd, 23–0002—23–4503; 29–0028—29–0243
Lockhart, John M., 42–0004—42–0231
Lockhart, John W., papers, 30–0197
Lockhart, Texas, 67–0080
Lockhart family, 79–0016
Lone Star Rifles, 74–0010
Long, James, 26–0392; 29–0028—29–0243
Long, Jane H., 23–0002—23–4503
Long, Lawrence, 72–0524—72–1992
Longfellow, Henry W., 24–0088; 79–0021
Longstreet, James, 79–0021
Looscan, Adele Lubbock Briscoe, 29–0028—29–0243; 35–0018—35–0122
Lotteries, 23–0002—23–4503
Loughery, Robert W., 29–0028—29–0243
Louisiana (steamship), 23–0002—23–4503
Louisville, Kentucky, 22–0023; 23–0002—23–4503; 32–0008; 51–0004—
    51–0125
Lount, William R., 25–0525—25–0552
Love, James, 23–0002—23–4503; 29–0028—29–0243; 46–0002; 52–0122;
    70–0475—70–0492; 73–0055—73–0341
Love, Mary F., 32–0008—32–0071
Love, Mrs. W. L., 62–0003—62–0200
Lovenberg, Isidore, 78–0017
Lovenberg Junior High School, records, 79–0034
Loving, Oliver, 29–0028—29–0243
Lowe, Robert G., 70–0200—70–0418
Lubben, John F., 29–0028—29–0243
Lubbock, Francis R., 35–0028—35–0122; 51–0004—51–0125
Lubbock, Henry S., 29–0028—29–0243
Lubbock, Thomas, 29–0028—29–0243
Lucas, J. C., 78–0022
Luce, Clare Boothe, 69–0243
Luckett, H. H., 74–0019
Ludecke, H., 22–0247
Ludlow, Israel L., 73–0055—73–0341
Lufkin, Walter E., 79–0013
Lufkin, Texas, 79–0011
Lumber trade, 23–0002—23–4503; 80–0004
Lumpkin, David P., 22–0247
Lutheran church, 23–0002—23–4503
Lutherloh, F. W., 74–0019

Lynch, William, 56–0005
Lynch & Savage, 70–0100—70–0162
Lynchburg, Texas, 23–0002—23–4503; 70–0100—70–0162
Lynchings, 41–0002—41–0005
Lynds, John, 44–0019
Lynn, Arthur Thomas, 23–0002—23–4503; papers, 49–0007—49–0013;
    73–0055—73–0341
Lynn & Williams, 23–0002—23–4503; 73–0055—73–0341
Lyons, Jane, 79–0013
Lyons, Louis J., 42–0232—42–0287
Lyon's Post Office, 23–0002—23–4503

Mass, Samuel, 23–002—23–4503; papers, 48–0007—48–0010; 70–0100—
    70–0162; 79–0011
McAlpin, W. K., 28–0005—28–0036
McArdle, Henry Arthur, 26–0372—26–0375; 27–0033—27–0039
McArdle, James, 22–0247
McArdle, Susan, 22–0247
McCane, Susan E., 38–0001
McCarthy, S. L., 79–0022
McCarty, John W., 70–0100—70–0162
McClellan, L. B., 77–0004
McClellan, W. B., slave deed, 38–0001
McClennan County, Texas, 23–0002—23–4503
McClosky, David, 22–0247
McClusky, F. Margarette, 14–0030
McCord, J. E., 74–0019
McCord, J. E., & Sons, 78–0017
McCord, Bowen & Lindsey, 78–0014
McCormick, Andrew Phelps, 35–0018—35–0122
McCrea, Susan E., letter, 31–1165
McCulloch, Ben, 29–0028—29–0243
McCulloch, Henry E., 29–0028—29–0243
McCulloch County, Texas, 78–0014
McCullough, John, 27–0019—27–0022; 49–0001—49–0006; 52–0019—
    52–0023; 52–0122; 70–1200—70–1258; 75–0016; 76–0039
McCullough, W. W., papers, 75–0016
McCutchan, Joseph D., diary, 72–0102—72–0103
McDade, William, 73–0055—73–0341
McDonald, Abner, 23–0002—23–4503; 29–0028—29–0243
McDonald, Angela, 52–0123
McDonald, J. E., 79–0021
McFarland, Thomas, 29–0028—29–0243
MacFarlane, Dugald, 29–0028—29–0243
McGahey, James S., 29–0028—29–0243
McGowan, Samuel, 25–0525—25–0552
McGregor, D., 23–4971—23–4993
McGregor, G. C., 73–0055—73–0341

McGregor, J. D., 77–0004
McHenry, John, 29–0028—29–0243
McKeen, A. C., 28–0102—28–0128
McKinney, Colin, 29–0028—29–0243
McKinney, H. C., 79–0014
McKinney, J. C., 74–0019
McKinney, James, 23–0002—23–4503
McKinney, Thomas F., 23–0002—23–4503; 29–0028—29–0243; 46–0002;
    73–0055—73–0341
McKinney, Groce & Company, 23–0002—23–4503
McKinney, Williams & Company, 23–0002—23–4503
McKinney & Menard, 23–0002—23–4503
McKinstry, George B., 23–0002—23–4503
McLean, Ephriam W., 23–0002—23–4503; 29–0028—29–0243; 73–0055—
    73–0341
McLean & Shannon, 77–0004
McLeary, James Harvey, 79–0014
McLemore, Marcus C., 78–0021; 79–0029
McLendon, S. G., 74–0019
McLennan County, Texas, 22–0247; 23–0002—23–4503
McLeod, Hugh, 23–0002—23–4503; 29–0028—29–0243
McMahan, F. W., 22–0153—22–0246
McMahan, T. H., & Company, 14–0030; 22–0247
McMahon & Gilbert, 78–0014
McMichael, David B., papers, 75–0014
McMillen, J. W., 23–0002—23–4503
McMinn, John, 04–0001—04–0007
McMullen, John, 29–0028—29–0243
McNaighen, I. S., 73–0055—73–0341
McNair & Company, 22–0247
McNeel, John Greenville, 22–0247
McNeel, Leander H., 23–0002—23–4503
McNeel, Manah, 22–0247
McNeel, Morgan L., 22–0247
McNeill, Mary C., 42–0004—42–0231
Macon, Mississippi, 22–0023
McRae, Colin J., 78–0014
McWillie, A. A., 73–0055—73–0341
Madden, J. W., 77–0029
Maddox, F. M. & J., 74–0019
Madero, J. Francisco, 23–0002—23–4503
Madison, James, 79–0021
Magale, J. F., 22–0247
Magazines, in early Texas, 23–0002—23–4503
Magee, Augustus William, 29–0028—29–0243
Magee, J. P., 22–0023
Mageean, Charlotte, 77–0004
Magnolia, Texas, 23–0002—23–4503; 70–0100—70–0162

Magnolia Grove Cemetery, records, 28–0293
Magruder, John Bankhead, 23–4920—23–4932; 25–0553—25–0567; 40–0002—40–0015b
Mahon, F. G., 74–0019
Mallard, John B., 42–0004—42–0231
Mallory, C. H., & Company, 28–0283
Mallory Steamship Line, 78–0014
Mallory strike, 1898, 52–0019—52–0023
Maloney, W. C., Jr., 22–0247
Manassas, Virginia, 74–0010
Maner, William, 23–0002—23–4503; 73–0055—73–0341
Mann, George E., 78–0014; 79–0013; 79–0024
Mann, Walter L., 22–0247
Mann & Baker, records, 79–0024
Manor, William, 73–0055—73–0341
Marburger, Marie, 79–0005; papers, 79–0020
Marcusy's Floating Docks, 47–0003—47–0028
Mardi Gras, 66–0042; 77–0005
Marion, Alabama, 70–0475—70–0492
Marks, J. W., 72–0524—72–1992
Markwell, Stubbs & Decker, 77–0024
Marlin, Texas, 27–0044—27–0699; 72–0524—72–1992; 74–0019
Marsh, Benjamin V., 78–0014
Marshall, William, 23–4971—23–4993
Martin, H. B., 23–0002—23–4503; 78–0009
Martin, L., 36–1202
Martin, Warrick, 23–0002—23–4503
Martin, Wylie, 23–0002—23–4503; 29–0028—29–0243
Martin, Carmona, Cruse, Micks & Dunten, 78–0023
Martin & Company, 23–0002—23–4503
Martinez, P. P., 78–0017
Martini, Minna, 79–0013
Martinsburg, Virginia, 74–0010
Marx, M., 56–0005; 80–0003
Marx & Kempner, 80–0002—80–0003
Mary Elizabeth (ship), 23–0002—23–4503; 72–0001
Mason, James, 22–0247
Mason, John Thompson, 23–0002—23–4503; 29–0028—29–0243
Mason, William, Jr., 22–0247
Masons. *See* Freemasonry
Massie, Charles W., 35–0018—35–0122; 74–0019
Massie, James Albert, 35–0018—35–0122
Masterson, A. R. and Branch T., 74–0019
Masterson, Rebecca, 23–5212
Masterson, Thomas G., 22–0247; 23–0002—23–4503; 23–5212
Matagorda, Texas, 23–0002—23–4503; 30–0850—30–0890; 40–0002—40–0015b; 70–0100—70–0162; 79–0014
Matagorda Bay, 23–0002—23–4503
Matagorda County, Texas, 30–0850—30–0890

Matamoros, Mexico, 23–0002—23–4503; 69–0274
Matry, James M., 51–0004—51–0125
Matt & Armstrong, 78–0014
Matthews, J. C., 74–0019
Matthews, John, 72–0524—72–1992
Matthews, Thomas R., 22–0023; 23–0002—23–4503
Maurer, Joseph M., papers, 74–0009
Maverick, Samuel Augustus, 29–0028—29–0243; 70–1200—70–1258
Maxey, Samuel Bell, 29–0028—29–0243; 70–0200—70–0418; 75–0004
Maxey, Thomas Sheldon, 74–0019
Mayer, R. A., 78–0014
Mayer, Kahn & Freiberg, 78–0014
Mayes, William Harding, 77–0004
Mayhoff, Gus, 78–0014
Maynard, N. I., 70–0425—70–0474
Medicine, 06–0005; 10–0001; 22–0009—22–0021; 22–0057—22–0152; 23–
    0002—23–4503; 27–0019—27–0022; 30–0197; 30–0892; 69–0247—
    69–0263; 79–0014; 79–0017—79–0018
Mellon, Sam W., journal, 28–0155
Melton, W. T., & Company, 78–0017
Memphis, Tennessee, 22–0023; 79–0011; 79–0029
Memple, George, 29–0028—29–0243
Memple, John, 29–0028—29–0243
Memple, William, 29–0028—29–0243
Menard, J. M. O., 76–0019
Menard, Michel Branamour, 23–0002—23–4503; 29–0028—29–0243; 46–
    0002; 51–0004—51–0125; residence, 65–0008; 72–1995; grant, 76–
    0024
Menard, Peter J., 23–0002—23–4503; 29–0028—29–0243; 52–0122; 72–
    0001
Menard, Pierre, 23–0002—23–4503
Menard, Peter J., & Company, 23–0002—23–4503
Menard & Leclerc, 23–0002—23–4503
Menardville, Texas, 74–0019
Menger, I. Simon N., 72–0524—72–1992
Mensing, G. H., 79–0013
Mensing, Walter B., 79–0013
Mensing & McCullough, 78–0009; 79–0013
Mensing & Thompson, 79–0013
Mensing Brothers & Company, 79–0013
Merchants, 67–0080; 69–0274; 70–0100—70–0162; 70–1200—70–1258;
    73–0055—73–0341; 74–0008; 79–0004; 79–0026; 80–0004. See also
    Commission merchants
Merchants & Manufacturers Lloyds Insurance Exchange, 78–0022
Merrick, Richard, 79–0021
Meridian, Texas, 70–0200—70–0418; 74–0019
Merriam, E. G., 70–0200—70–0418
Merriman, F. H., 23–0002—23–4503; 73–0055—73–0341
Mexia, Texas, 74–0019

Mexican citizenship, for Texans, 23–0002—23–4503
Mexican cypress, 23–0002—23–4503
Mexican government of Texas, 23–0002—23–4503; 23–5210
Mexican War, 31–1178; 50–0001; 74–0018
Mexico (steamer), 23–0002—23–4503
Meyer, Anna, 36–1202
Meyer, G. A., 78–0014
Meyer, Ludwig, 60–0002
Meyer, Margaretha Dorothea Sophia, 60–0002
Meyer family, papers, 60–0002
Michael, S. C., & Company, 33–0041—33–0093
Mier expedition, 50–0415; 72–0102—72–0103
Mier y Teran, Juan de, 23–0002—23–4503
Mier y Teran, Manuel de, 23–0002—23–4503
Mikado Club, 76–0016
Milam, Benjamin R., 23–0002—23–4503; 29–0028—29–0243
Milam County, Texas, 23–0002—23–4503
Milbank, Robert W., 23–0002—23–4503
Milbank, J. & R., Company, 23–0002—23–4503
Milbank, R. W., & Company, 23–0002—23–4503
Milburn, William, 72–0524—72–1992
Military affairs, 23–0002—23–4503; 26–0372—26–0375; 27–0033—27–
    0039; 31–1178; 70–1271—70–1272; 77–0030
Mill, C. C., Elevator & Light Company, 77–0004
Millard, Henry, 29–0028—29–0243; 70–0425—70–0474
Miller, Dale, 71–0386
Miller, James B., 23–0002—23–4503; 29–0028—29–0242
Miller, James Francis, 70–0200—70–0418
Miller, Roy, 71–0386
Millis, Robert, 73–0055—73–0341
Mills, Albert N., 27–0044—27–0699
Mills, Andrew, 50–0001
Mills, D. O., 70–0200—70–0418
Mills, John T., 29–0028—29–0243
Mills, Robert, 23–0002—23–4503; 29–0028—29–0243
Mills, A. G. & R., 23–0002—23–4503
Mills, R., & Company, 23–0002—23–4503
Mills, R. & D. G., 23–0002—23–4503; 74–0019
Mills and milling, 23–0002—23–4503
Mills & Trevis, 22–0247
Mills County, Texas, 56–0005; 77–0004; 78–0014
Mina, Xavier, 29–0028—29–0243
Mining in Texas, 23–0002—23–4503
Minor, Alice, 22–0023
Minor, Berkley, 22–0023
Minor, E. G., 77–0004
Minor, F. D., 78–0014
Minor, John B., 22–0023
Minor, Launcelot, 22–0023

Minor, Lucian, 22–0023; 46–0002; 78–0014
Minot, James Alexander, 70–0035; 76–0016
Minot, Kendall J., 76–0016
Minot, Willie Ida, 76–0016
Minot family, papers, 76–0016
Mississippi Colony, 23–0002—23–4503
Mistrot family, 78–0017
Mitchell, Asa, 23–0002—23–4503; 29–0028—29–0243; 51–0004—51–0125
Mobile, Alabama, 23–0002—23–4503; 23–4909—23–4919; 28–0293; 32–0008; 36–0045—36–1201
Mokes & Brother Company, 33–0041—33–0093
Moller, Jens, 56–0005; 78–0014
Monahans, Texas, 78–0017
Monclova, Mexico, 23–0002—23–4503
Money market, 23–0002—23–4503
Money scarcity, 23–0002—23–4503
Monroe, James, 70–0425—70–0474; 79–0021
Montague, Daniel, 29–0028—29–0243
Montgomery, Sarah Ann, 70–0100—70–0162
Montgomery, J. S., & Company, 78–0014
Montgomery, Alabama, 22–0247; 23–0002—23–4503; 25–0553—25–0567
Montgomery County, Texas, 23–0002—23–4503; 42–0004—42–0231; 56–0005; 72–0524—72–1992; 78–0014; 78–0017
Moodie, S. O., 70–0200—70–0418
Moody, William L. III, 44–0007—44–0015
Moody, William Lewis, 28–0233; 70–0200—70–0418; papers, 78–0014
Moody, W. L., & Company, 78–0014; 79–0012
Moody family, 76–0027
Moody Foundation, 71–0387
Moore, Bartlett D., 76–0019
Moore, Edwin Ward, 23–0002—23–4503; 29–0028—29–0243; letter, 33–0001; 72–0001; 74–0018
Moore, Francis, Jr., 23–0002—23–4503; 29–0028—29–0243
Moore, Hugh B., papers, 78–0022
Moore, James L., 77–0004
Moore, John, 29–0028—29–0243; 70–0475—70–0492; 71–0376—71–0383
Moore, John H., 23–0002—23–4503; 29–0028—29–0243
Moore, Philip, 27–0006—27–0012
Moore, Thomas O., 25–0525—25–0552; 32–0008
Moore & McKinstry, 23–0002—23–4503
Moore & Parker, 22–0247
Moorefield, Virginia, 22–0023
Morel, A. R., 28–0293
Morello, Mary, 78–0014
Morey, P. T., 76–0016
Morgan, George Dickinson, 80–0007
Morgan, James, 23–0002—23–4503; 29–0028—29–0243; papers, 31–0001—31–1096; 31–1231—31–1243
Morgan, Jean Scrimgeour, 19–0027; 80–0007

Morgan, John D., 51–0004—51–0125
Morgan, Leon A., 81–0007
Morgan, W. C., 74–0019
Morgan, William Manning, 80–0007; papers, 80–0008
Morgan family, papers, 80–0007
Mormon Mill Colony, 71–0376—71–0383
Morning Light (ship), 77–0002
Moro Castle, 72–1995
Morphy, Diego, 36–0002
Morrell, Z. N., 29–0028—29–0243
Morris, Suzanne, papers, 76–0022
Morse, Samuel F. B., 79–0021
Morticians, 71–0390
Moser, Hyacinth, 79–0026
Moser, Paula, 79–0026
"Mosquito fleet," 79–0037
Motley, William, 29–0028—29–0243
Mott, Marcus F., 23–0002—23–4503
Mount Vernon, Texas, 25–0525—25–0552
Muldoon, Michael, 23–0002—23–4503; 25–0001—25–0521; 29–0028—29–0243
Muller & Broderson, 22–0247
Mullin, Texas, 74–0019
Munger, E. I., 72–0524—72–1992
Murrah, Pendleton, 40–0002—40–0015b
Murray, Oscar G., 51–0004—51–0125
Murphy, Edward, 29–0028—29–0243
Music, 30–0198; 75–0017; 76–0011
Musick, H. T., 22–0247
Musquiz, Melchor, 23–0002—23–4503
Musquiz, Miguel, 23–0002—23–4503
Musquiz, Ramon, 23–0002—23–4503
Mussina, Simon, 23–4909—23–4919
Mussina vs. *Moore*, 23–0002—23–4503
Mustang (ship), 49–0014—49–0021
Muster rolls, 30–0197; 36–0003—36–0009; 40–0002—40–0015b; 42–0004—42–0231; 51–0004—51–0125; 70–0425—70–474; 77–0011
Mutinies, 33–0001
Mutscher, Gus, 78–0023
Myers, L. S., 70–0425—70–0474
Myrtle Vale, Texas, 70–1150—70–1178

Nacogdoches, Texas, 23–0002—23–4503; 35–0018—35–0122
Nance, Joseph Milton, 72–0102—72–0103
Napp, Fred, letter, 76–0026
Napp, Maggie, 76–0026
Naschke, Bertram B., 79–0005
Nash, B. H., 23–0002—23–4503
Nash, Cicero, 23–0002—23–4503

Nash, James P., 23–0002—23–4503; 27–0044—27–0699
Nashville, Tennessee, 23–0002—23–4503; 25–0525—25–0552
Nast, Thomas, 79–0021
Natchez, Mississippi, 23–0002—23–4503; 32–0008; 36–0045—36–1201
Natchitoches, Louisiana, 23–0002—23–4503; 36–0045—36–1201
Native Americans, 31–1165; 79–0017
Navarro, Jose Antonio, 23–0002—23–4503; 29–0028—29–0243
Navarro County, Texas, 79–0014
Navasota, Texas, 22–0247; 33–0041—33–0093; 51–0004—51–0125; 72–0524—72–1992
Naylor, Henrietta Wood, 35–0018—35–1022; 79–0010
Naylor, Isaac, 79–0010
Naylor family, papers, 79–0010
Neblett, Robert C., 51–0004—51–0125
Neblett, Sterling, 46–0002; 51–0004—51–0125
Neill, Andrew, 29–0028—29–0243; 70–1271—70–1272
Neitche, Theodore, 71–0385
Nesbitt, Robert, 76–0023
Newark, New Jersey, 23–4920—23–4932
New Bedford, Massachusetts, 79–0011
New Braunfels, Texas, 23–0002—23–4503; 33–0041—33–0093; 36–1202
New Braunfelser Zeitung, 29–0028—29–0242
New Haven, Connecticut, 70–0475—70–0492
New Orleans, Louisiana, 22–0023; 22–0247; 23–0002—23–4503; 24–0088; 25–0525—25–0552; 28–0293; 32–0008; 33–0001; 36–0003—36–0009; 36–0045—36–1201; 42–0004—42–0231; 51–0004—51–0125; 66–0042; 67–0080; 69–0274; 70–0100—70–0162; 71–0385; 72–0001; 72–0524—72–1992; 73–0055—73–0341; 74–0018; 79–0019
Newscome, J. C., 72–0524—72–1992
Newspapers, 23–0002—23–4503; 79–0017
Newton, Mrs. H. M., 35–0018—35–0122
Newton, Joseph, 70–0200—70–0418
New York, 32–0008; government, 76–0037; 79–0019
New York & Texas Land & Securities Syndicate, 78–0014
New York & Texas Steamship Company, 78–0014
New York City, 22–0247; 23–0002—23–4503; 76–0037
New York Tribune, 24–0088
New York Volunteers, 175th, 77–0002
Neyland & Douglas, 77–0004
Nicholls, George B., 32–0008
Nichols, Ebenezar B., 23–0002—23–4503; 28–0102—28–0128; 40–0002—40–0015b; 52–0122
Nichols, J. N., 23–0002—23–4503
Nichols, Mollie, 74–0010
Nichols, Samuel P., 79–0021
Nicol, Francis, 79–0020
Niigata, Japan, 79–0028
Niigata Committee, records, 79–0028
Niles, T. N., 23–0002—23–4503

Nimmo, Joseph, Jr., 70–0200—70–0418
Noble, William H., Jr., 29–0028—29–0243
Nolan, Philip, 29–0028—29–0243; 35–0018—35–0122
Nolan, Thomas H., 68–0039; 68–0057—68–0074
Nolan County, Texas, 78–0014
Norman, A. P., 76–0019
Northern, Mary Moody, 71–0387
Northers, 23–0002—23–4503
Norton, H. D., 70–0100—70–0162
Norvell, Lipscomb, 29–0028—29–0243
Novels, 76–0022; unfinished, 29–0244
Nuclear ships, 75–0013
Nurseries, 23–0002—23–4503
Nussbaum, H., 80–0002—80–0003

Oakland plantation, 23–0002—23–4503
Obion, Tennessee, 70–0100—70–0162
O'Brien, G. W., 78–0017
O'Brien, Hannah, 14–0030
Ochiltree, Thomas P., 29–0028—29–0243; 70–0200—70–0418
Ochiltree, William B., 29–0028—29–0243
O'Connell, Daniel Pius, papers, 74–0002
O'Connor, Laing & Smoot, 78–0014
Odin, J. M., 29–0028—29–0243; 46–0002; 69–0274
O'Driscoll, Jack, 42–0232—42–0287
O'Halloran, Charles, 79–0020
Ohmstede, Theodore, 79–0014
Oil and gas. See Petroleum
Old Custom House, Galveston, 77–0003
Oldham, Williamson Simpson, 25–0525—25–0552; 29–0028—29–0243
Oleander Festival, 77–0005
Oleanders, 37–0003; 77–0005
Oliver, David T., family notes, 71–0196
Ollre family, 79–0016
Olmsted, Frederick Law, Jr., 78–0019
Onderdonk, Andrew, 70–0200—70–0418
Oneida County, New York, 36–0045—36–1201
Opera, 76–0017—76–0018
Oppenheimer, L., 33–0041—33–0093
Oppermann, William, 79–0011
Orange County, Texas, 56–0005; 78–0014
Order of Chosen Friends, 75–0004
Organists. See Organizations, musical
Organizations:
—art, 52–0123
—benevolent, 36–1205—36–1207; 78–0021; 80–0006
—cultural, 75–0008
—historical, 77–0003; 78–0003
—horticultural, 79–0007

—literary, 30–0199; 67–0021—67–0022; 80–0005
—musical, 30–0198; 48–0080; 75–0007—75–0015; 76–0011; 78–0011
—relief, 14–0030; 19–0027; 62–0201; 79–0015
—service, 38–0003; 80–0006
—social, 30–0895; 51–0126; 66–0042; 77–0021—77–0022; 79–0007
—theatrical, 78–0011; 78–0026
Orizaba (vessel), 25–0525—25–0552
Orphanages. *See* Children
Ort, Johan, 79–0013
Ort, William, 79–0013
Orthmann, A., 79–0011
Orynski, L., 79–0014
Orynski, Thompson & Company, 79–0014
Oser, Mildred M., 79–0020
Osterman, Joseph, 23–0002—23–4503; 46–0002
Osterman Widows & Orphans Home Fund, records, 79–0031
Oswald, Theodore, & Company, 79–0011
Otey, James H., 32–0008
Overland, G., 70–0100—70–0162
Overton, William, 22–0023
Owen, Clark L., 23–0002—23–4503; 29–0028—29–0243
Owen, John, 23–0002—23–4503; 74–0018
Owen, Nellie, 22–0023; 23–5212
Owenville, Texas, 22–0247; 72–0524—72–1992
Oysters, 23–0002—23–4503

Pabst, Elvira Adriance, 78–0017
Pacific Express Company, 78–0014
Padilla, Juan Antonio, 23–0002—23–4503; 29–0028—29–0243
Palestine, Texas, 23–0002—23–4503; 70–0100—70–0162
Palmer, Edward A., 72–0524—72–1992
Palmetto Hotel, 77–0004
Palo Pinto County, Texas, 78–0014
Papenheim, Albert, 36–1202
Pardee, E. H., 70–0200—70–0418
Paretti, Mayo, 76–0019
Paris, France, 32–0008; 69–0274
Paris, Texas, 28–0293; 70–0200—70–0418
Park, F. M., 78–0014
Park, Mrs. S. S., letter, 28–0052
Parker, Daniel, 29–0028—29–0243
Parker, Isaac, 29–0028—29–0243
Parker, W. E., 29–0028—29–0243; 51–0004—51–0125
Parker & Flippen, 22–0247
Parmer, Martin, 29–0028—29–0243
Parr, Samuel, 77–0004
Parsons, B. S., 23–0002—23–4503; 70–0163—70–0170; 76–0019
Parsons, Frank, 79–0011
Pascal, D. A., 77–0004

Paschal, George Washington, 29–0028—29–0243
Pass Christian, Mississippi, 32–0008
Pastell, Miguel, 69–0274
Patents, 47–0003—47–0028
Patillias, ———, 23–0002—23–4503
Patrick, George, 23–0002—23–4503; 29–0028—29–0243
Patrick, Walter A., 22–0247
Patten, Frank C., 29–0028—29–0243; 35–0018—35–0122; papers, 78–0019; 79–0020
Patton, C. R., 22–0153—22–0246; 23–0002—23–4503
Patton, E. O., 22–0153—22–0246
Payne, Susan E., 70–0100—70–0162
Peabody, George, 79–0021
Peach Land, Texas, 42–0004—42–0231
Peak, Donald T., 79–0020
Pearson, P. E., 74–0019
Pease, Elisha Marshall, 23–0002—23–4503; speech, 70–0017
Pease, Mrs. L. C., 74–0019
Peck, George R., 28–0233
Peckham, S. F., 32–0005
Peebles, Robert, 23–0002—23–4503; 29–0028—29–0243
Peeler, Henry A., 28–0061—28–0101
Pendexter, George F., 75–0004
Pendleton, Henry, 77–0003
Penland, Samuel M., autograph album, 79–0021
Pera, Juan de, 79–0021
Percy, H. R., 24–0007—24–0035
Perigueux, France, 69–0274
Perkins, Nancy, 42–0004—42–0231
Perote, Mexico, 72–0102—72–0103
Perry, Mrs. Elton, 79–0013
Perry, Henry, 29–0028—29–0243
Pershing, John J., 78–0022
Petersburg, Virginia, 22–0057—22–0152; 23–0002—23–4503
Petroleum, 24–0068—24–0070; 32–0005; 40–0027; 77–0029; 78–0017
Pettibone, Louise F., 51–0004—51–0125
Pettus, John F., 29–0028—29–0243
Pettus, William, 23–0002—23–4503; 29–0028—29–0243; 73–0055—73–0341
Pfister & Vogel Leather Company, 79–0011
Phelps, James Aeneas E., 23–0002—23–4503; 29–0028—29–0243
Phelps, Orlando C., 29–0028—29–0243
Phelps, Virgil A., 29–0028—29–0243
Phelps & Willrich, 78–0014
Philadelphia, Pennsylvania, 23–0002—23–4503; 36–0045—36–1201; 70–0200—70–0418; 79–0011
Phillips, Alexander H., 70–1200—70–1258
Phillips, Dan, 28–0005—28–0036
Phillips, L. C., 24–0007—24–0035

Phillips, Moro, 23–0002—23–4503
Phillips, William, 30—0850–30–0890
Phipps, E. G., 70–0425—70–0474
Photography and photographers, 74–0009; 76–0003
Physicians. *See* Medicine
Pickering, John, 29–0028—29–0243
Piedras, Jose, 23–0002—23–4503
Pierce, Charles C., 35–0018—35–0122
Pierce, Franklin, 79–0021
Pierson, Sarah E., 78–0009
Pike, John A., 77–0004
Pike, S. M., 28–0293
Pilant, Palmer Job, 70–0425—70–0474
Pilant, T. W., 77–0003
Pilgrim, Thomas J., 23–0002—23–4503; 29–0028—29–0243; 35–0018—35–0122
Pillsbury, Timothy, 29–0028—29–0242
Pilots, 75–0002
Pilsbury, Charles A., 35–0018—35–0122
Pine Bluff, Arkansas, 70–0200—70–0418
Pintado, Vicente Sebastin, 44–0019
Pitts, William A., 29–0028—29–0243
Plain Dealing, Louisiana, 22–0247
Plantations and planters, 23–0002—23–4503
Plata Piedra Mining Company, 78–0014
Pleasant, W. A., 72–0524—72–1992
Pleasanton, Texas, 28–0293; 74–0019
Plentitude, Texas, 22–0153—22–0246
Plumly, B. Rush, 27–0044—27–0699; 28–0061—28–0101; 70–0200—70–0418
Plumm, G. W., 70–0100—70–0162
Plunkett, John, 30–0850—30–0890
Poetry, 23–5212; 30–0197; 35–0005—35–0016; 51–0004—51–0125; 71–0199—71–0206; 74–0010
Poindexter, J. J., 51–0004—51–0125
Political broadsides and circulars, 76–0019
Politics, Galveston, 04–0066; 23–0002—23–4503; 27–0044—27–0699; 27–0702; 28–0293; 36–0003—36–0009; 76–0019; 76–0023; 76–0042; 78–0023—78–0024; 79–0006; 79–0022
Politics, Texas, 04–0049—04–0050; 04–0066; 23–0002—23–4503; 50–0001; 70–0017; 75–0004; 78–0023—78–0024
Polk, James K., 79–0021
Polk, Leonidas, 25–0553—25–0567
Ponton, Andrew, 29–0028—29–0243
Ponton, William, 29–0028—29–0243
Pope, Captain John, 75–0016
Poplar Hill, Virginia, 22–0057—22–0152
Porrer, Thomas B., 73–0055—73–0341
Port Arthur, Texas, 62–0003—62–0200; 79–0020

Porter, Fitz John, 79–0021
Port Isabel, Texas, 71–0326—71–0370
Port Lavaca, Texas, 23–0002—23–4503; 70–0100—70–0162
Port of Galveston. *See* Galveston, Port of
Ports, Mexican, 23–0002—23–4503
Postal service, 23–0002—23–4503
Potomac (ship), 72–0001
Potter, Henry N., 51–0004—51–0125
Potter, M. H., 78–0014
Potter, M. M., 51–0004—51–0125
Potter, Robert, 29–0028—29–0243; 72–0001
Potter, Reuben M., 74–0018
Powell, Elizabeth, 30–0850—30–0890
Powell, Samuel G., 30–0850—30–0890
Powhattan House Hotel, Galveston, 72–1995; 79–0007
Prairie View A & M University, 04–0049—04–0050; 79–0005
Prentiss, S. S., 79–0021
Presbyterian church, 23–0002—23–4503; 70–0163—70–0170; 72–1995; 76–
    0039; 78–0014
Prescott, W. H., 79–0021
Preston, C. W., 06–0005
Preston, Texas, 30–0850—30–0890
Preston & Robira, *Physician's Dose List*, 06–0005
Prevost, Anne, 36–0045—36–1201
Prevost, Augustine, 36–0045—36–1201
Prevost, Jacob, 36–0045—36–1201
Priaer, Dennis, 33–0001
Price, James W., 28–0293
Price, L. B., 22–0023
Prichard, Margaret Johnston, 35–0018—35–0122
Priestly, William, letter, 69–0243
Prince Edward County, Virginia, 22–0057—22–0152
Pringle, James R., 22–0023
Prisoners of war, 50–0415; 69–0243
Pritchard, Henry, 29–0028—29–0243
Programs, 75–0017; 76–0017—76–0018; 78–0011
Promissory notes, 23–0002—23–4503
Providence, North Carolina, 42–0004—42–0231
Providence Press and Star, 24–0088

Quigg, W. P., 28–0102—28–0128
Quincy, Massachusetts, 79–0019
Quintana, Texas, 23–0002—23–4503; 72–0001

Ragsdale, J. T., 78–0017
Ragsdale, Silas B., papers, 79–0030
Raguet, Anna, 28–0295
Railroads, 04–0066; 22–0247; 23–0002—23–4503; 24–0007—24–0035; 25–

Roemer, J. B., 79–0026
Rhodes, E. A., 25–0001—25–0521
Rhodes, William H., 70–0475—70–0492
Rice, Edwin E., journal, 36–0041
Rice, Thomas Geale, papers and scrapbook, 62–0003—62–0200; 62–0202
Rice, Baulard & Company, 78–0014
Richards, J. W., 70–0200—70–0418
Richardson, D., 27–0044—27–0699
Richardson, Sid, 78–0017
Richardson, Willard, 23–0002—23–4503; 29–0028—29–0243
Richardson, Belo & Company, 24–0088
Richmond, Texas, 23–0002—23–4503; 30–0850—30–0890; 72–0524—72–1992; 74–0019
Richmond, Virginia, 23–0002—23–4503; 23–4920—23–4932; 25–0553—25–0567; 22–0023; 72–0524—72–1992
Richmond County, Georgia, 36–0045—36–1201
Ricker, Florence Harris, 75–0005
Ricker, John Romaine, 75–0005
Ricker, Nathaniel, 75–0005
Ricker, Norman Hurd, 75–0005
Riddell, J. W., Banker, 78–0025
Riddell & Pettit, 78–0014
Riley, J. M., 74–0019
Rinker, Selim, 22–0247
Rio Arriba County, New Mexico, 28–0293
Ripon College, 78–0019
Roach, Matthew, 78–0014
Robbins, William, 23–0002—23–4503; 72–0001
Robert, Henry M., 22–0024
Roberts, John H., 29–0028—29–0243
Roberts, Oran Milo, letters, 04–0049—04–0050
Roberts, S. A., 29–0028—29–0243
Robertson, Annie Dowling, 35–0018—35–0122
Robertson, David R., 70–0425—70–0474
Robertson, Elijah Sterling Clack, 29–0028—29–0243
Robertson, Jerome, 29–0028—29–0243
Robertson, John C., 25–0525—25–0552; 29–0028—29–0243
Robertson, Sawnie R., 29–0028—29–0243
Robertson County, Texas, 78–0014
Robinson, George E., 76–0019
Robinson, James W., 29–0028—29–0243
Rodents, and health, 79–0009
Rodney, Michigan, 36–0045—36–1201
Rodriguez, Policarpo, 29–0028—29–0243
Roeck family, 69–0247—69–0263
Roemer, Edward, 70–0200—70–0418
Rogers, J. F., 23–0002—23–4503
Rogers, W. K., 24–0088
Rogers, William L., 29–0028—29–0243

154

Rogers, Texas, 74–0019; 78–0017
Rogers Ranch, 78–0017
Rogerville, Tennessee, 04–0001—04–0007
Rojas, Ramon Garcia, 23–5210
Rolison, Joel W., 29–0028—29–0243
Roman Catholic church, 23–0002—23–4503; 72–1993; 74–0002
Roper, Ben E., 22–0023
Rose, N. P., 29–0028—29–0243
Rosenberg, Henry, 23–0002—23–4503; 32–0008; 33–0097; 40–0002—40–0015b; 72–1995; 77–0004; 78–0009; 78–0014; 78–0025; 79–0005; 79–0012
Rosenberg, Letitia Cooper, 33–0097; 77–0004
Rosenberg, Mary Ragan Macgill ("Mollie"), 33–0097
Rosenberg family, papers, 33–0097; 78–0009; 78–0014
Rosenberg, H., & Company, 23–0002—23–4503
Rosenberg Bank, papers, 78–0009; ledgers and journal, 78–0025; letter-press volumes, 78–0027
Rosenberg Library, 15–0001; 40–0027; 67–0021—67–0022; scrapbooks, 76–0033; 78–0003; 78–0019; papers, 79–0005; 79–0020
Rosenberg Women's Home, 29–0244; records, 74–0001; 79–0005
Rosenfield, J., 51–0004—51–0125
Ross, Lawrence Sullivan, 70–0200—70–0418
Ross, S. P., 79–0013
Ross, Shapley P., 20–0028—29–0243
Rotary Club of Galveston, records, 38–0003
Rothenstein, Frank S., 25–0525—25–0552
Routen, Joseph Hall, 22–0247
Rovers Rest, Texas, 42–0004—42–0231
Rowe, Samuel, 23–0002—23–4503; 73–0055—73–0341
Royal Yacht (schooner), 53–0001
Rucker, W. W., 72–0524—72–1992
Ruhl, Louisa, 27–0044–27–0699
Ruiz, Francisco, 23–0002—23–4503
"Runaway Scrape," 28–0052
Runge, Henry J., 56–0005
Runge, J. Forrest, 56–0005
Runge, Johanna, 56–0005
Runge, Louis H., 56–0005
Runnels, Hiram George, 23–0002—23–4503; 73–0055—73–0341
Runnels County, Texas, 78–0014
Rusk, Thomas Jefferson, 23–0002—23–4503; 29–0028—29–0243; 35–0018—35–0122; 49–0001—49–0006; 79–0021
Rusk, Texas, 70–1150—70–1178; 79–0014
Russell, William Jarvis, 23–0002—23–4503; 29–0028—29–0243
Rygaard, Kincy, 68–0158

Sabin, Chauncey Brewer, 22–0153—22–0146
Sabine County, Texas, 51–0004—51–0125
Sabine Pass, Texas, 23–0002—23–4503; 70–0100—70–0162

Sabo, Herman, 28–0005—28–0036
Saengerfest (Texas State Singing Society), 56–0005
St. Cyr, Henri de, 23–0002—23–4503; 27–0044—27–0699
St. Denis, Louis Juchereau de, 29–0028—29–0243
St. John, Caroline, 23–0002—23–4503
St. John, Howell William, 23–0002—23–4503
St. John, Samuel, Jr., 23–0002—23–4503
St. John, Sophia Williams, 23–0002—23–4503
St. John, William Henry, 23–0002—23–4503
St. John, Chidsey & Company, 23–0002—23–4503
St. John & Tousey, 23–0002—23–4503
St. Josephs' Catholic Church, 72–1995
St. Louis, Sallie Lee, 75–0005
St. Louis, Missouri, 22–0023; 32–0008; 69–0274; 70–0200—70–0418; 79–
    0019
St. Mary's Cathedral, Galveston, 74–0002
St. Mary's Seminary, La Porte, Texas, 74–0002
St. Mary's University, 78–0014
St. Paul's German Presbyterian Church, 76–0039
St. Stephens, Alabama, 79–0019
Sampson, Edwin, 72–0524—72–1992
Sampson, George, 72–0524—72–1992
Sampson, Henry, 23–0002—23–4503; papers, 69–0266—69–0273; 72–
    0524—72–1992
Sampson, Peter Gray, 72–0524—72–1992
Samuel, R. J., 73–0055—73–0341
San Angelo, Texas, 74–0019; 79–0019
San Antonio (ship), 33–0001; 72–0001
San Antonio, Texas, 22–0023; 22–0247; 23–0002—23–4503; 27–0044—27–
    0699; 28–0293; 30–0850—30–0890; 33–0041—33–0093; 36–1202;
    70–0100—70–0162; 70–0200—70–0418; commerce, 70–1200—70–
    1258; 72–0524—72–1992; 79–0014; 79–0019
San Antonio Drug Company, 79–0014
San Augustine, Texas, 79–0027
San Augustine County, Texas, 23–0002—23–4503; 51–0004—51–0125
San Bernard (ship), 72–0001
San Bernard River, 23–0002—23–4503
Sanborn, Mrs. Lloyd F., Jr., 79–0020
San Felipe (ship), 23–0002—23–4503; 72–0001
San Felipe de Austin, 22–0247; 23–0002—23–4503
San Francisco, California, 79–0020
San Jacinto, Battle of, 25–0525—25–0552; 26–0372—26–0375; 27–0033—
    27–0039
San Jacinto, Texas, 23–0002—23–4503
San Jacinto (ship), 33–0001; 72–0001
San Luis, Texas, 23–0002—23–4503; 70–1179—70–1189
San Luis Company, records, 70–1179—70–1189
Sanderson, D. D., 74–0019
Sandusky, William H., 46–0002

Sandy Creek, 23–0002—23–4503
Sanford, Fred E., 70–1150—70–1178
San Patricio, Texas, 22–0247; 23–0002—23–4503; 69–0274; 70–1271—70–1272
San Saba County, Texas, 78–0014
Santa Anna, Antonio Lopez de, 23–0002—23–4503; 26–0372—26–0375; 27–0033—27–0039
Santa Anna (vessel), 23–0002—23–4503
Santa Fe, New Mexico, 28–0293
Santa Fe expedition, 51–0004—51–0125
Santa Fe Railroad, 23–0002—23–4503; 77–0004
Sartvelle, W. L., 74–0019
Sarvis, J. S., 79–0013
Sarwold, Albert N., 69–0243
Sass, Harry B., 32–0008
Saturday Evening Civilian, 29–0028—29–0243
Sauer, Mrs. F. C., 62–0003—62–0200
Saunders, Alvin, 78–0014
Sauters, John, 23–0002—23–4503; 28–0102—28–0128; estate papers, 30–0028—30–0196; 52–0122; 78–0009
Savannah (ship), 75–0013; 75–0014
Sawyer, Philetus, 79–0021
Saxe, J. G., 79–0021
Sayers, Joseph D., 29–0028—29–0243
Sayles, Henry, 70–0200—70–0418; 74–0019; 77–0004
Sayre, Charles D., 23–0002—23–4503; 67–0080
Scates, Alexander Washington, 23–4902—23–4908
Scates, Charles Keyser, 23–4902—23–4908
Schackelford family, letters, 76–0038
Schadt, Charles, 74–0010
Schadt, William F., 74–0010
Schadt family, papers, 74–0010
Schaefer & Koradi, 79–0011
Scheidt, Otto, 56–0005
Schleicher, Gustav, 29–0028—29–0243
Schlutter & Blanton, Lumber, cashbook, 80–0004
Schmidt, L. W., 79–0011
Schoolfield, Isaac, 79–0011
Schools. *See* Education
Schott, Christine, 76–0001
Schott, Justus Julius, family history, 76–0001
Schreiner, Charles, 28–0293
Schroeder, Charles, 78–0014
Schuberth, Edward, 79–0011
Schwartz, Aaron Robert ("Babe"), papers, 78–0024
Scott, George W., 23–0002—23–4503
Scott, Mary Jane, 23–0002—23–4503
Scott, N. B., 79–0021
Scott, Thomas F., 74–0019

Shannon, Alexander M., & Company, 28–0061—28–0101
Sharman, Robert, 51–0004—51–0125
Sharp, L., 79–0027
Sharp, William, 27–0044—27–0699; 73–0055—73–0341
Shaul, W. A., 29–0028—29–0243
Shaw, Frank D., 29–0028—29–0243
Shaw, George Charles, 79–0021
Shaw, James B., 23–0002—23–4503
Shaw, James R., 73–0055—73–0341
Shaw, John B., 74–0019
Shaw, Joshua, 73–0055—73–0341
Shaw, Robert Wallace, 75–0005
Shay, W. E., 76–0019
Sheldon, F. L., 78–0014
Sheldon, Henry, 77–0003
Sheldon, J. C., 27–0044—27–0699
Shepherd, B. A., 23–0002—23–4503
Shepherd, D. P., 35–0018—35–0122
Sheppard, Abraham and Elenor, 30–0850—30–0890
Sheppard, W. C., 72–0524—72–1992
Sheriff's sales, 23–0002—23–4503
Sherman, Catherine Isabella, 25–0525—25–0552
Sherman, Sidney, 23–0002—23–4503; papers, 25–0525—25–0552; 28–0102—28–0128; 29–0028—29–0243
Sherwood, John P., 22–0247; 23–0002—23–4503
Sherwood, Lorenzo, scrapbook, 04–0066; 23–0002—23–4503
Shields, James A., 35–0018—35–0122
Shiloh, Battle of, 23–4920—23–4932
Ships and shipping, 22–0153—22–0246; 33–0014—33–0020; 48–0007—48–0010; 49–0014—49–0021; 75–0001—75–0002; 75–0013—75–0014; 76–0016; 77–0013
Shoemakers, 23–0002—23–4503
Shorter, John Gill, 79–0021
Shreveport, Louisiana, 25–0553—25–0567
Shriver, J. L., 32–0008
Shriver, Samuel S., 32–0008
Shropshire & Company, 22–0247
Sigurney, Mrs. ———, 79–0021
Siles, Mrs. Earnestine, 28–0295
Silver mining, 23–0002—23–4503
Simpson, Mrs. B., 78–0014
Simpson, D., 23–0002—23–4503
Simpson, J. H., 32–0008
Simpson, W. L., 73–0055—73–0341
Simpton, George, 46–0002
Sims, F., 25–0525—25–0552
Sims, H. T., 74–0019
Sims & Wright, 77–0004
Sinclair, John G., 62–0003—62–0200

Sinclair, W. H., 75–0004; 78–0014
Sintenis, Emil H., 74–0019
Sjolander, John Peter, papers, 35–0005—35–0016
Skinner, J. D., 78–0014
Slavery, 23–0002—23–4503; 23–4909—23–4919; 23–4920—23–4932; 23–5212; 27–0041; 28–0047—28–0051; 30–0197; 30–0850—30–0890; 33–0004—33–0012; 38–0001; 41–0002—41–0005; 44–0006; 50–0001; 51–0004—51–0125; 69–0274; 71–0326—71–0370
Sledge, Lunceford A., 30–0850—30–0890
Sledge, R. J., 70–0200—70–0418
Sledge Realty Company, 77–0003
Sleight, John L., 22–0153—22–0246; 23–0002—23–4503
Small, Matthew, 70–0200—70–0418
Smally, E. V., 24–0088
Smith, Ashbel, 29–0028—29–0243
Smith, Benjamin Fort, 29–0028—29–0243
Smith, Calvin S., 23–0002—23–4503
Smith, Charles B., 22–0023
Smith, Edward Kirby, 25–0553—25–0567
Smith, Erastus ("Deaf"), 29–0028—29–0243
Smith, H. D. W., 28–0293
Smith, Henry, 26–0372—26–0375; 46–0002; 72–0001
Smith, J. P., 22–0247
Smith, J. Mason, 72–1995
Smith, James, 29–0028—29–0243
Smith, John W., 35–0018—35–0122
Smith, Leon, 25–0525—25–0552
Smith, Nathan, 72–0001
Smith, Niles F., 70–0100—70–0162
Smith, R. K., 22–0247
Smith, Robert, 70–0200—70–0418
Smith, Robert K., 27–0044—27–0699
Smith, Will, 77–0004
Smith, J. F., & Brother, records, 74–0008
Smith County, Texas, 79–0013
Smithwick, Edward, papers, 71–0376—71–0383
Smithwick, Noah, 29–0028—29–0243
Smyth, George W., 23–0002—23–4503; 29–0028—29–0243
Smyth, Henry M., 51–0004—51–0125
Society for Friendless Children, 78–0021
Somervell, Alexander, 23–0002—23–4503; 29–0028—29–0243; 70–1200—70–1258
Somervell County, Texas, 22–0247
Somervell expedition, 70–0510—70–1138
Somerville, Albert, 28–0293; 32–0008
Sommer, Adolph, 36–1202
Sonoita Valley Land & Colonization Company, 79–0011
Sons of the American Revolution, 78–0019
Sorley, James, 23–0002—23–4503; 72–0524—72–1992

Sour Lake, Texas, 23–0002—23–4503; 70–0100—70–0162
South Bosque, Texas, 27–0044—27–0699
Southern Cotton Press Company, 78–0014
Southern Investment Company, 78–0022
Southern Methodist University, 78–0023
Southern Pacific Company, 44–0016; 46–0002
South Galveston & Gulf Shore Railroad, 78–0014
South Texas National Bank, 30–0896; 80–0001
South Texas State Bank, 78–0025
Southwestern University, 78–0023
Southwick, Sandford B., 23–4909—23–4919
Southwick, Stephen, 23–0002—23–4503; 23–4909—23–4919; 52–0122
Spanish-American War, scrapbooks, 76–0044
Spann, Eleanor, 70–0100—70–0162
Sparks, S. F., 29–0028—29–0243
Spartan Mill Company, 70–0100—70–0162
Speassing, John F., 70–0200—70–0418
Specie, 23–0002—23–4503
Speirs, M. N., 78–0014
Spencer, F. M., 78–0014
Spencer, William, 73–0055—73–0341
Spillane, Richard, 22–0023
Spofford, Susan, 78–0014
Spotsylvania County, Virginia, 22–0247
Spring, Texas, 79–0011
Spring Branch, Texas, 23–0002—23–4503
Springfield, Kentucky, 30–0850—30–0890
Springfield, Texas, 72–0524—72–1992
Stafford, J. B., 77–0004
Stafford, W. M., 29–0028—29–0243
Stamped paper, 23–0002—23–4503
Stanley, Delilah, 22–0247
Stapp, Darwin M., 29–0028—29–0242
"Star money," 23–0002—23–4503
Starr, James Harper, 29–0028—29–0243
Stavenhagen, Ernest III, scrapbooks, 75–0017; 77–0047
Stavenhagen, Ernest Charles, 77–0047
Stavenhagen, Ernst Gottlieb, 77–0047
Stavenhagen family tree, 77–0047
Stead, J. B. & J. W., 74–0019
Steamboats, 23–0002—23–4503
Steele, Alphonso, 29–0028—29–0243
Steele, O., 28–0102—28–0128
Steffens, Otto W., 74–0019
Stein, Beverley Walden, 71–0199—71–0206
Stephens, Alexander H., 79–0021
Stephens, J. F., 23–0002—23–4503; 72–0001
Stephens County, Texas, 78–0014
Sterett, William Greene, 29–0028—29–0243

Sterne, Adolphus, 29–0028—29–0243
Sterns, C. H., 23–0002—23–4503; 70–0100—70–0162
Stevens, J. C., 70–0425—70–0474
Stevens, J. W., 35–0018—35–0122
Stevens, William H., 70–1150—70–1178
Stewart, Alexander P., 25–0553—25–0567
Stewart, Charles, 70–0200—70–0418
Stewart, Charles Bellinger, 26–0372—26–0375; 29–0028—29–0243
Stewart, F. Nichols, 79–0012
Stewart, J. S., 26–0372—26–0375
Stewart, John, 73–0055—73–0341
Stewart, Maco, 78–0014; 78–0017; 79–0014
Stewart Title Guaranty Company, 78–0019
Stickney, E. Lawrence, 23–0002—23–4503
Stiefel, Lucy, 79–0020
Stigler, G. W., 74–0019
Stillings, Sallie, 42–0004—42–0231
Stockfleth, Julius, 73–0342
Stockfleth, Mrs. W. P., letters, 73–0342
Stone, Mrs. C. B., 79–0013
Stone, Mildred Richards. *See* Gray, Millie
Story, A. C., 32–0008
Stowe, H. B., 79–0021
Stowe, W. N., 78–0014
Stowe, William N., Jr., 49–0014—49–0021
Straight, W. E., 22–0247
Street, R. G., 70–0200—70–0418; 78–0014; 79–0005
Strobel, Lewis M., 73–0055—73–0341
Strong, W. B., 28–0233
Stroud, Beden, 72–0524—72–1992
Strussy & Blum, 78–0025
Stuart, Ben C., 29–0028—29–0243
Stuart, H. C., 79–0005
Stuart, Hamilton, 23–0002—23–4503; 29–0028—29–0243
Stuart, J. C., 70–0200—70–0418
Stubbs, James B., 76–0019
Stubbs, James B. and Charles J., papers, 75–0004
Stubbs, Theodore B., mayoral papers, 77–0024; 79–0006
Sugar, 23–0002—23–4503; 33–0004—33–0012e; 80–0003
Sullivan, C. C., 79–0027
Sulzer, William, scrapbook, 76–0037
Surveyors and surveying, 23–0002—23–4503
Sutherland, George, 23–0002—23–4503; 29–0028—29–0243
Sutton, John S., 29–0028—29–0243
Swartwout, Samuel, 31–0001—31–1096; 31–1231—31–1243
Swartwout, Texas, 23–0002—23–4503; 70–0100—70–0162
Sweet, Ada P., 77–0014
Sweet, Eliza Williams, 23–0002—23–4503
Sweet, George, 23–0002—23–4503

Swingle, Alfred, 70–0425—70–0474
Swisher, John G., 29–0028—29–0243
Swisher, John Milton, 23–0002—23–4503; 29–0028—29–0243
Sydnor, John S., 23–0002—23–4503; 25–0001—25–0521; 46–0002
Sydnor, Seabrook W., 78–0014
Sylvester, James Austin, papers, 26–0372—26–0375

Talfor, Robert B., 24–0088
Talleyrand, Charles Maurice de, 80–0009
Tampico, Mexico, 23–0002—23–4503; 69–0274
Tampico expedition, 36–0003—36–0009
Tarrant, Edward H., 29–0028—29–0243
Tarrant County, Texas, 78–0014
Taxes and taxation, 23–0002—23–4503; 30–0997; 77–0004
Tayler, H. D., 42–0004—42–0231
Taylor, E. W., 23–0002—23–4503; 28–0293
Taylor, Edward, 29–0028—29–0243
Taylor, J. M., 79–0014
Taylor, James, 23–0002—23–4503; 36–0045—36–1201; 56–0005
Taylor, Thurston M., 72–0001
Taylor, William M., 52–0122
Taylor, Zachary, 23–0002—23–4503; 49–0007—49–0013
Teal, Henry, 23–0002—23–4503; 29–0028—29–0243
Teiwes, Oscar, 79–0005
Temple, Texas, 28–0233
Temple, B'Nai Israel, 79–0033
Tennessee, emigrants from, 23–0002—23–4503
Tennille, George, 23–0002—23–4503
Tenoxtitlan, Texas, 23–0002—23–4503
Terrell, Alexander Watkins, 29–0028—29–0243
Terrell, Charles M., 70–0100—70–0162
Terrell, Edward S., 35–0018—35–0122
Terrell, J. C., 35–0018—35–0122
Terrell County, Texas, 56–0005
Terry, Benjamin, 29–0028—29–0243
Terry, John Wharton, 29–0028—29–0243
Terry, Nat, 29–0028—29–0243
Terry & Ballinger, 78–0014
Terry's Texas Rangers, 25–0553—25–0567; 71–0326—71–0370
Texana, Texas, 23–0002—23–4503
Texas (steam dredge), logbook, 32–0066; 70–0035
Texas (steamship), 23–0002—23–4503; 76–0016
Texas:
—annexation, 77–0012
—attorney general, 23–0002—23–4503
—Cavalry, Eighth Regiment, 1861–65, 25–0553—25–0567; 71–0326—71–0370
—commerce, 23–0002—23–4503; 63–0002; 71–0386
—comptroller, 23–0002—23–4503

Thaliseul, Gustave, 79–0011
Thames, R. I., slave deed, 44–0006
Thayer, H. S., 28–0061—28–0101
Theater, in Galveston, 76–0016—76–0018; 78–0011; 78–0026
Theobald, Charles H., 76–0019
Thomas, John C., 30–0850—30–0890
Thomas, Sallie A., 42–0004—42–0231
Thomas, W. B., 78–0017
Thomason, T. T., 74–0019
Thompson, Abigail, 79–0019
Thompson, Alexander, 23–0002—23–4503; 72–0001
Thompson, Charles E., 28–0102—28–0128
Thompson, Clark W., 76–0027; 79–0020
Thompson, Cyrus, 79–0019
Thompson, E. E., 30–0850—30–0890; 79–0014
Thompson, Ellen Emily, 79–0014
Thompson, Ellen Graves, 30–0850—30–0890
Thompson, Isham, papers, 30–0850—30–0890; 79–0014
Thompson, J. A., 35–0018—35–0122
Thompson, J. E., 42–0004—42–0231
Thompson, James Edwin, papers, 69–0247—69–0263
Thompson, Libbie Moody, papers, 76–0027
Thompson, Margaret P., 78–0009; 79–0013
Thompson, Robert A., 35–0018—35–0122
Thompson, Smith, 79–0021
Thompson, Thomas, 23–0002—23–4503; 30–0850—30–0890
Thompson, Thomas C., papers, 79–0014
Thompson, Texas, 42–0004—42–0231
Thompson & Ohmstede, 78–0025; 79–0014
Thompson Drug Company, 79–0014
Thorn, Frost, 23–0002—23–4503; 29–0028—29–0243
Thornberry, Texas, 35–0018—35–0122
Thornton, E. H., Jr., ferry records, 69–0276
Thornton, J. E., 24–0088
Thorpe, Edward, 52–0122
Thurston, Algernon Sidney, 23–0002—23–4503; 72–0001
Tichenor, Stephen W., 23–0002—23–4503; 73–0055—73–0341
Tiernan, R. H., 79–0008
Tiffany, Ann C., 73–0055—73–0341
Timber Ridge, Virginia, 35–0018—35–0122
Times, A. F., 73–0055—73–0341
Timon, John, 29–0028—29–0243
Titcomb, Albert, 78–0009
Titus, Andrew Jackson, 29–0028—29–0243
Toby, Thomas, 23–0002—23–4503; 72–0001
Toby's Express, 23–0002—23–4503
Tod, John Grant, 23–0002—23–4503; 72–0001; papers, 74–0018
Toebelman, Elizabeth Jersig, 79–0011
Toebelman, John Henry, 79–0011

Toebelman family, papers, 79–0011
Toland, Emily, 42–0004—42–0231
Toland, T. F., 42–0004—42–0231
Tolands Depot, Mississippi, 42–0004—42–0231
Toledo, Jose Alvarez, 29–0028—29–0243
Tolstoi, Count Lev, 28–0295
Tom, H. S., 28–0293
Tom, John Files, 29–0028—29–0243
Tombstones, 23–0002—23–4503
Tom Toby (ship), 72–0001
Torrey, David K., 29–0028—29–0243
Torrey, George B., 29–0028—29–0243
Torrey, James A., 29–0028—29–0243
Torrey, John F., 29–0028—29–0243
Torrey, Judson, 29–0028—29–0243
Torrey, Stephen, 29–0028—29–0243
Torrey, Thomas S., 29–0028—29–0243
Townes, Robert J., 23–0002—23–4503; 73–0055—73–0341
Trans-Mississippi Commercial Congress, 79–0012
Travel, description, 28–0155; 30–0197; 50–0437; 76–0038
Travis, William Barret, 22–0247; 23–0002—23–4503; 29–0028—29–0243
Travis County, Texas, 23–0002—23–4503; 40–0002—40–0015b; 51–0004—
        51–0125; 56–0005; 78–0014
Treaccer, Mrs. K. M., 78–0009
Treaccer family, 78–0009
Tremont Hotel, 23–0002—23–4503
Tremont Opera House, programs, 76–0018
Trenton, New Jersey, 22–0247; 28–0293
Trimble, R. C., 22–0023; 46–0002
Trinity, Texas, 78–0023
Trinity Episcopal Church, papers, 79–0001. *See also* Episcopal church
Trinity River, 23–0002—23–4503
Triplett, Robert, 51–0004—51–0125
Trube house, 72–1995
True Blue, 51–0004—51–0125
Trueheart, Charles W., 23–0002—23–4503; 78–0017
Trueheart, Henry Martyn, family papers, 22–0023; 23–0002—23–4503;
        78–0012; 78–0014
Trueheart, O., 23–0002—23–4503
Trueheart, H. M., & Company, 72–1995; letterpress volumes, 78–0012;
        ledgers, 78–0013; papers, 78–0014
Trust, Thomas, 73–0055—73–0341
Tucker, Anna, 77–0003
Tucker, H. A., 23–0002—23–4503
Tucker, Hiram, 23–0002—23–4503
Tucker, Isabella T., 77–0003
Tucker, Louis O., 77–0003
Tucker, Mary Cecelia, 77–0003

Urrea, Jose de, 23–0002—23–4503
Ursuline Academy, Galveston, 23–0002—23–4503; 72–1995
Ursuline Convent of Galveston, 71–0162
Urwitz, Marie Bennet, 35–0018—35–0122
Utilities, 77–0019
Uvalde, Juan de, 29–0028—29–0243

Valle, Santiago del, 23–0002—23–4503; 23–5210
Van Alstyne, A. A., 76–0019
Van Buren, Martin, 23–0002—23–4503
Van Sickle, Stephen, 23–0002—23–4503; 70–0425—70–0474
Van Zandt, Isaac, 23–0002—23–4503; 29–0028—29–0243
Vaughn, G. W., 62–0003—62–0200
Veers, John Henry, papers, 30–0997
Velasco, Texas, 23–0002—23–4503; 51–0004—51–0125; 70–0475—70–0492; 72–0001
Velocity (ship), 77–0002
Vera Cruz, Mexico, 23–0002—23–4503
Veramendi, Juan Martin, 23–5210
Verbeke, A., & Company, 70–1287
Vergennes, Vermont, 77–0003
Vicksburg, Mississippi, 22–0023; 23–0002—23–4503
Victoria, Texas, 22–0247; 23–0002—23–4503; 71–0386
Vidor, King Wallis, letter, 77–0014
Viesca, Jose Maria, 23–0002—23–4503; 23–5210
Viesca, Juan A., 56–0005
Viesca syndicate, 56–0005
Vincent, Peter Ames, 78–0026
Vineyards, 23–0002—23–4503
Virginia Land Company, 78–0014
Virginia Point, Texas, 23–4920—23–4932; 40–0002—40–0015b; 42–0004—42–0231
Visit to Galveston Island in 1818, A, 27–0041
Vocke, Louis, 36–1202
Volunteerism, 80–0006
Vowinckle, William, 79–0013

Waco, Texas, 27–0044—27–0699; 51–0004—51–0125; 70–0200—70–0418; 70–0475—70–0492; 71–0326—71–0370; 79–0013; 79–0015
Wadican, W., 79–0021
Wager, David, 22–0247
Wagner, H. W., 36–0003—36–0009
Wagner, Thomas, 79–0026
Wagoners, 23–0002—23–4503
Wakelee, David, Jr., 23–0002—23–4503; 28–0005—28–0036
Walbridge, Elbridge, 23–0002—23–4503; 70–0475—70–0492; papers, 71–0385
Walker, A. J., 79–0012
Walker, George J. S., 36–0045—36–1201

Walker, James, 51–0004—51–0125
Walker, John C., 23–0002—23–4503; 78–0014
Walker, Mamie Ketchum, letter, 65–0008
Walker, Robert J., 36–0045—36–1201
Walker, Samuel Hamilton, 29–0028—29–0243
Walker, Tipton, 23–0002—23–4503; 28–0005—28–0036
Walker, John N., & Company, 33–0041—33–0093
Walker, Kent & Company, 22–0247
Wallace, A., 42–0004—42–0231
Waller, Edwin, 23–0002—23–4503; 29–0028—29–0243
Waller, Hiram B., 23–0002—23–4503; 29–0028—29–0243
Wallis, John C., 42–0002—42–0231
Wallis, Joseph Edmund, 42–0004—42–0231
Wallis, Landes & Company, 28–0233
Wallis family, papers, 42–0004—42–0231
Walmsley, Lewis R., 25–0001—25–0521
Walnut Ridge, Arkansas, 70–0200—70–0418
Walthew, Mrs. B. O., 79–0013
Walton, George, 56–0005
Walton, William M., 29–0028—29–0243
Ward, Thomas William, 23–0002—23–4503; 29–0028—29–0243
Ward & Martin, 79–0005
Ware, James T., 23–0002—23–4503
Ware, Nathaniel A., 27–0044—27–0699; 73–0055—73–0341; 79–0019
Ware, Robert J., 22–0247
Ware, William B., 46–0002
Warfield, Catherine A., 27–0044—27–0699; 79–0019
Warfield, E., 27–0044—27–0699
Warfield, N. W., 27–0044—27–0699
"Warloope" Victoria, 23–0002—23–4503
Warmoth, Mrs. W., 79–0020
Warnekon & Kirchoff, 23–0002—23–4503
War of 1812, 04–0001—04–0007
Washington, Booker T., 28–0295
Washington, D.C., 22–0023; 23–0002—23–4503; 24–0088; 74–0018; social life, 76–0027; 79–0019
Washington, Texas, 23–0002—23–4503; 25–0525—25–0552; 30–0197; 30–0850—30–0890; 70–0100—70–0162; 72–0001; 72–0524—72–1992; 73–0055—73–0341; 77–0012
Washington County, Texas, 23–0002—23–4503; 33–0004—33–0012; 22–0247; 56–0005
Waterman, L. E., & Company, 78–0019
Waters, James S., 29–0028—29–0242
Watrous, John C., 23–0002—23–4503; 23–4909—23–4919; 29–0028—29–0243
Watson, John P., 51–0004—51–0125
Watson, Margaret L., 35–0018—35–0122
Watson, Nellie, letter, 48–0103
Watterson, Henry, 79–0021

Waul, Thomas Neville, 29–0028—29–0243
Waul's Legion, 36–0041
Waxahachie, Texas, 72–0524—72–1992
Weather, 73–0381
Weatherford, Texas, 72–0524—72–1992; 74–0019
Webb, James, 23–0002—23–4503; 29–0028—29–0243
Webb, Walter Prescott, 71–0387
Weber, Retta Lou Stavenhagen, 77–0047
Weber, William, 46–0002
Webster, Daniel, 79–0021
Wednesday Club, records, 77–0028
Wegner, Ernest C., 79–0011
Weis, Leopold, 78–0014
Weis Brothers, 78–0014
Weiss, William and Napoleon, letters, 31–1180—31–1183
Wells, Clinton G., papers, 24–0007—24–0035; 70–0200—70–0418
Wells, P. T., 72–0001
Wells, Lysander, 23–0002—23–4503; 70–1271—70–1272
Wells, R. B., & Company, 78–0014
Wells, Texas, 79–0014
Welsh & Brother, 22–0153—22–0246
Werlin, Rosella Horowitz, 77–0005
Werner, William, 22–0247
West, Hamilton A., papers, 30–0896
West Columbia, Texas, 23–0002—23–4503; 70–0475—70–0492; 72–0001;
    74–0019; 79–0015
West End Improvement Company, 78–0014
Westerlage, John H., 22–0247; 23–0002—23–4503
Westervelt, P. D., 78–0014
Westhafer, E. K., 42–0232—42–0287
Weston, Daniel, 79–0019
Westrope, Fannie, 79–0019
Westrope, Frances, 79–0019
Wharton, Clarence Ray, 35–0018—35–0122
Wharton, Edward C., 25–0525—25–0552
Wharton, John Austin, 23–0002—23–4503; 23–4909—23–4919; papers,
    25–0553—25–0567; 29–0028—29–0243; 72–0001; 75–0004
Wharton, Penelope Johnson, 25–0553—25–0567
Wharton, William Harris, 23–0002—23–4503; 29–0028—29–0243
Wharton, Texas, 30–0850—30–0890; 51–0004—51–0125; 73–0055—73–
    0341; 79–0014
Wharton County, Texas, 23–0002—23–4503; 30–0850—30–0890
Wharton (ship), 72–0001
Wheeler, Kate Baker, 35–0018—35–0122
Wheeler, Royal Tyler, 29–0028—29–0243
Wheelwright, George Washington, 23–0002—23–4503; 72–0001
Whipple, George M., 51–0004—51–0125
White, Clement B., 22–0247

White, Daniel O., 22–0247
White, Edward D., 27–0006—27–0012
White, Joseph, 23–0002—23–4503
White, Mary S., 22–0247
White, N. A., 27–0044—27–0699
White, Sam Addison, 70–0100—70–0162
White, Walter C., 23–0002—23–4503
White, Zebulon Lewis, papers, 24–0088
White, Walter C., & Company, 23–0002—23–4503
Whitelaw, Reid, 24–0088
Whitesill, Barbara, 04–0001—04–0007
Whiting, G. R. A., 72–0524—72–1992
Whiting, Isaac, 78–0017
Whiting, Sam, 23–0002—23–4503; 30–0850—30–0890
Whitney, Texas, 74–0019
Whittier, C. G., 56–0005
Whittier, John G., 79–0021
Whitting, George, 56–0005
Wichita County, Texas, 78–0014
Wigfall, Louis Trezevant, 29–0028—29–0243
Wightman, Elias R., 23–0002—23–4503
Wilbarger, Josiah Pugh, 23–0002—23–4503; 29–0028—29–0243
Wilbur, A. C., 22–0023
Wilder, E., 28–0233
Wilkens, Richard B., 30–0895
Willard, W. R., 76–0019
Willia, R. S., 51–0004—51–0125
William Penn (steamer), 70–0100—70–0162
Williams, Augustus, 23–0002—23–4503; 29–0028—29–0243
Williams, Austin May, 23–0002—23–4503; 73–0055—73–0341
Williams, C. D., 23–0002—23–4503
Williams, C. J., 76–0019
Williams, Caroline Lucy, 23–0002—23–4503
Williams, Dorothy Wheat, 23–0002—23–4503
Williams, Eliza, 23–0002—23–4503
Williams, Ezekiel, 23–0002—23–4503
Williams, George L., 23–0002—23–4503
Williams, Henry Howell, 23–0002—23–4503; 46–0002; papers, 73–0055—
    73–0341
Williams, Jennie Sylvester, 26–0372—26–0375; 27–0033—27–0039
Williams, Job, 23–0002—23–4503
Williams, John A., 23–0002—23–4503
Williams, John H., 23–0002—23–4503; 27–0044—27–0699
Williams, John R., 23–0002—23–4503
Williams, John Wilkins, 73–0055—73–0341
Williams, Joseph Guadalupe Victoria, 23–0002—23–4503
Williams, Marjorie A., article, 70–0005
Williams, Mary Anna Adams, 23–0002—23–4503

Williams, Mary Dorothea, 23–0002—23–4503
Williams, Matthew Reed, 23–0002—23–4503
Williams, Nathaniel Felton, 23–0002—23–4503; 73–0055—73–0341
Williams, Nathaniel Felton, the elder, 23–0002—23–4503
Williams, O. H., 23–0002—23–4503; 73–0055—73–0341
Williams, Parker, 23–0002—23–4503
Williams, Price, 32–0008
Williams, Rebecca Wilkins, 23–0002—23–4503
Williams, Robert H., 23–0002—23–4503
Williams, Samuel May, papers, 23–0002—23–4503; 23–4997—23–5198; 27–0041; 28–0005—28–0036; 28–0293; 29–0028—29–0243; 33–0004—33–0012; 36–0003—36–0009; 51–0004—51–0125; 70–0475—70–0492; 70–1200—70–1258; 73–0055—73–0341; 74–0028; 77–0003
Williams, Samuel May, Jr., 23–0002—23–4503
Williams, Sarah Patterson Scott, 23–0002—23–4503
Williams, William Howell, 23–0002—23–4503; 73–0055—73–0341
Williams, H. H., & Company, 23–0002—23–4503
Williams, John H. & Henry H., 23–0002—23–4503; 73–0055—73–0341
Williams, Joseph V., & Company, 23–0002—23–4503
Williams, Whitman & Company (New Orleans), 23–0002—23–4503
Williams & Bates, 23–0002—23–4503
Williams & Browning, 23–0002—23–4503
Williams & Menard, 23–0002—23–4503
Williams Building, 72–1995
Williamsburg, Virginia, 22–0023
Williams Depot, Texas, 72–0524—72–1992
Williamson, M. B., 73–0055—73–0341
Williamson, Marcus, 70–0425—70–0474
Williamson, R. F. ("Dick"), 76–0019
Williamson, Robert McAlpin, 22–0247; 23–0002—23–4503; 29–0028—29–0243
Williamson, General T. T., 23–0002—23–4503; 73–0055—73–0341
Williamson, W. S., 72–0001
Williamson & Andrews, 71–0385
Williams-Tucker House, 72–1995
Willie, James, 73–0055—73–0341
Willie, Campbell & Ballinger, 78–0014
Willis, Albert S., 70–0200—70–0418
Willis, J. B., 79–0014
Willis, J. E., 46–0002
Willis, Peter J., 79–0005
Willis, R. M., 79–0013
Willis, R. S., 70–0200—70–0418
Willis, William H., 79–0005
Willis, P. J., & Brother, 23–0002—23–4503; 78–0014
Wilmington, Delaware, 32–0008
Wilmington, North Carolina, 42–0232—42–0287
Wilson, Eliza, 67–0080
Wilson, George W., 67–0080

172

Wilson, Henry T., 28–0061—28–0101; 67–0080
Wilson, James, 23–0002—23–4503; 29–0028—29–0243; 51–0004—51–0125
Wilson, Robert, 23–0002—23–4503; 29–0028—29–0243
Wilson, Theodore O., papers, 67–0080; 77–0003
Wilson, Will, 65–0002
Wilson, William F., 25–0001—25–0521
Wimhurst, Anna Moser, 79–0026
Wimhurst, Frederick, Jr., 79–0026
Wimhurst, George A., 79–0026
Wimhurst family, papers, 79–0026
Wimmer, O. E., 79–0011
Winkler, C. M., 29–0028—29–0243; 72–0524—72–1992
Winkler, Ernest William, 29–0028—29–0243
Winne, Gilbert, 77–0003
Winnie, G. Albert, 23–4971—23–4993
Winston, George T., 79–0014
Winterbotham, John Miller, 79–0033; autograph collection, 34–0033
Wise County, Texas, 78–0014
Withers, J. M., 25–0553—25–0567
Wittig, Hattie, 52–0123
Wolston, R. W., 76–0019
Wolston, Wells & Vidor, 24–0007—24–0035
Woman suffrage, 75–0019
Women, in politics, 69–0275; 78–0028
Women's Choral Club of Galveston, records, 48–0080
Women's Civic League, records, 37–0003
Women's Health Protective Association, 36–0045—36–1201; 37–0003
Women's homes, 74–0001
Women's organizations, 36–0045—36–1201; 37–0003; 48–0080; 51–0126;
    77–0028
Wood, Francis A., 22–0057—22–0152
Wood, Henry Augustine, papers, 22–0057—22–0152
Wood, James D., 22–0057—22–0152
Wood, W. D., 72–0524—72–1992
Woodlawn plantation, Virginia, 22–0247
Woods, William, 22–0247
Woods Bluff, Texas, 42–0004—42–0231
Woods Cross, Utah, 28–0293
Woodson, Goodridge, 22–0023
Wooten, Dudley, 75–0004
Worland, Charles R., 30–0850—30–0890
World War I, homefront, 19–0027; 38–0003; 78–0022
World War II, 38–0003; 69–0243; 72–0111—72–0308; 72–0310; 72–1993;
    76–0023; 78–0022
Wortham, J. C., 78–0014
Wortham Auditorium, 79–0005
Wright, G. E., 79–0014
Wright, George W., 29–0028—29–0243
Wright, Irene A., 27–0700

Wright, John F., 73–0055—73–0341
Wright, Travis G., 29–0028—29–0243
Wright, William H., 23–0002—23–4503; 73–0055—73–0341
Wurzbach, Harry McLeary, 79–0012
Wyse, William, 72–0001

Yarborough, Ralph W., 71–0387
Yard, E. T., 28–0293
Yard, Emory Neal, 28–0293
Yard, Nahor Biggs, 14–0030; 22–0023; 23–0002—23–4503; 28–0102—28–
    0128; papers, 28–0293; 32–0041; 33–0014—33–0020; 33–0021—33–
    0023; 36–0003—36–0009
Yard, William L., 28–0293
Ybarra, Jesus Maria, 23–0002—23–4503
Yellow fever, 14–0030; 23–0002—23–4503; 30–0892; 41–0002—41–0005;
    44–0001; 67–0080
Yoakum, Henderson, 29–0028—29–0243
Youens, Jesse, 29–0028—29–0243
Young, Frank, 28–0295
Young, Gustave, 22–0247; 23–4971—23–4993
Young, William C., 29–0028—29–0243
Young County, Texas, 78–0014
Young Men's Christian Association, 33–0097; 78–0019; 79–0005
Young Women's Christian Association, 80–0015
Yves, Andrieux, 42–0232—42–0287

Zahn, Caroline, 76–0003
Zahn, Elise Kreppett, 76–0003
Zahn, Franz, 76–0003
Zahn, Justus, 76–0003
Zahn family, papers, 76–0003
Zapata, Antonio, 29–0028—29–0243
Zaruba, J., 79–0011
Zavala, Adina de, 29–0028—29–0242; 35–0018—35–0122
Zavala, Lorenzo de, 23–0002—23–4503; 29–0028—29–0243; 35–0018—
    35–0122
Zavalla County, Texas, 78–0014
Zavalla (ship), 72–0001
Ziegler, J., 62–0003—62–0200
Ziegler, Jesse A., 35–0018—35–0122
Zork, L., 56–0005
Zuber, William Physick, 29–0028—29–0243

174